The Final
Testament

The Two Witnesses

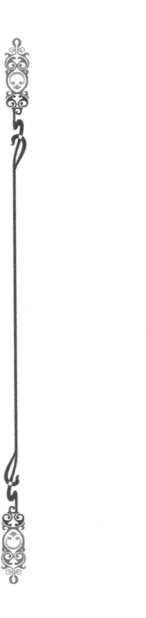

Revealed by: ~ *Holy Spirit* ~

Inspired by: *Apostle John*

Written by: *Ima Prophet*

~ *Preword* ~

To the scholar's of this world who read this testament in its volume, I should say. As I had noted in the beginning of the writings called "before hand". That there were a number of things that had not been revealed at the time of the writings. To this cause you will find what appears to be errors or contradictions, but they are not. If you wait upon the Holy Spirit to guide you though these areas you will then find the depth of its meaning and know the correct interpretation as He, The Holy Spirit gave it in its time of revealing. As a man, such as yourself, I desired to change it as I came to understand more concerning it. But the Spirit of Truth would not let me, because it is His Works, not mine. And it is His understanding and intent that will accomplish what was done and is being done and what is yet to come. To this cause I have not changed any part of what was written in that day nor have I taken a single word from it. Therefore I added an expansion in the area of the Seals for those, like myself who find a need to connect all these things which have occurred, to the present time and understanding of the world and its history as we know it. Just as the Scribes of past times have added to the scriptures for this same cause .To this end do I pray for all who read this testament to find the patience of the Saints as to the understanding of all these things. For there have been many before us and also some in the days to follow who will not wait upon the Lord or His Council and to this cause will add sorrows onto themselves that need not be. But the Lord and His tender and loving mercies are for our weaknesses that we should not condemn ourselves concerning all these things. Therefore pray and wait for the understanding and you shall have it. Look not in the council of men for answers, but in the depth of your heart where the Lord and the Holy Spirit do dwell. Now here is Wisdom. Handle the Word of God with the Fear of God in all Tremblings. Because He is God.......

Order this book online at www.trafford.com
or email orders@trafford.com

Most Trafford titles are also available at major online book retailers.

Printed in Victoria, BC, Canada.

ISBN: 978-1-4251-2568-4

*Our mission is to efficiently provide the world's finest, most comprehensive
book publishing service, enabling every author to experience success.
To find out how to publish your book, your way, and have it available
worldwide, visit us online at www.trafford.com*

Trafford rev. 11/13/2009

www.trafford.com

North America & International
toll-free: 1 888 232 4444 (USA & Canada)
phone: 250 383 6864 ◆ fax: 812 355 4082

~ *Content* ~
Writings of a Prophet / 2005
(Testament)

Writings of a Prophet / 1982

(Before hand)

Revelation Prophecies

~ *Foreword* ~

As it is written in Revelation 10:8

8 And the voice which I heard from heaven spake unto me again, and said, Go and take the little book which is open in the hand of the angel which standeth upon the sea and upon the earth. 9 And I went unto the angel, and said unto him, Give me the little book. And he said unto me, Take it, and eat it up; and it shall make thy belly bitter, but it shall be in thy mouth sweet as honey. 10 And I took the little book out of the angel's hand, and ate it up; and it was in my mouth sweet as honey: and as soon as I had eaten it, my belly was bitter. 11 And he said unto me, <u>Thou must prophesy again before many peoples, and nations, and tongues, and kings</u>.

For this cause I say to you in this book of testament is this prophesy being fulfilled in your sight. For I tell you a truth, the Spirit of John has come unto you in this the last days. And it was concerning these things when it was said in John 21:23.

23 Then went this saying abroad among the brethren, that that disciple should not die: Yet Jesus said not unto him, He shall not die; but, If I will that he tarry till I come, what is that to thee? 24 This is the disciple which testifieth of these things, and wrote these things: and we know that his testimony is true. 25 And there are <u>also many other things which Jesus did</u>, the which, if they should be written every one, I suppose that even the world itself could not contain the books that should be written

Amen......

For as it is written, "Thou <u>must</u> prophesy again". Therefore, it <u>must</u> come forth. Consider also Rev. 20: 6 Blessed and holy is <u>he</u> that hath part in the <u>first resurrection</u>: <u>on such</u> the <u>second death</u> hath <u>no power</u>, but <u>they</u> shall be <u>priests</u> of <u>God</u> and of <u>Christ</u>, and shall reign with him a thousand years. It is through this saying that John is <u>prophesying again</u>. And in like manner did Elias (Elijah) come under the name of John the Baptist. That is to say, he came in <u>Spirit</u> and was <u>one</u> with him. As the Lord said concerning John the Baptist: Matt. 11:9

11:9 But what went ye out for to see? <u>A prophet</u>? yea, I say unto you and <u>more than a prophet</u> 10 <u>For this is he of whom, it is written</u>, Behold, I send my messenger before thy face, which shall prepare thy way before thee. 11 Verily I say unto you, Among them that are born of women there hath not risen a <u>greater than John the Baptist</u>: notwithstanding he that is least in the kingdom of heaven is greater than he. 12 And <u>from</u> the <u>days</u> of <u>John</u> the <u>Baptist</u> <u>until now</u> the <u>kingdom</u> of <u>heaven</u> "<u>suffereth violence</u>", and the <u>violent take it</u> by <u>force</u>. 13 For all the prophets and the law prophesied until John. 14 And if ye will receive it, <u>this is Elias, which was for to come</u>. 15 He that hath ears to hear, let him hear. **And as John the Baptist (Elijah)** was the fulfilling of the prophecy of the Great Day of the Lord and its coming so also is this Testament the fulfilling of the prophecy of John the Apostle in the Last Days and the Great Rapture in its coming. Let not these sayings trouble you, but rather comfort you for in it came the fullness of our Salvation.

Amen and Amen..

The majority of this testament was written in nineteen eighty two and eighty three (1982-83).Then the Lord said : Seal up this testament for many days and go and live the days which I have added unto you, until I return and finish the work which I have given you. For it will be your generation that I will accomplish the works there in. And in that day shall they know that I have spoken these words unto you...

Amen and Amen.......

All this began in Alexandria, Virginia when I was nine years old when the Lord gave me two (2) separate dreams in one night. First I should say, I don't remember dreams nor can I close my eyes and see images as most people do. To this cause I was very moved and excited and woke up immediately after each dream. The first dream was concerning the earth and the inhabitants there of. I saw the earth from above as it would be seen from a satellite. It was beautiful ! Keep in mind that this was in nineteen fifty five (1955). As I watched the earth make a complete rotation it began to change and the blue sky became a reddish brown. and the waters became greenish brown.. On the next revolution it changed again. This time it had no oceans and little water. And the ground was parched and cracked. And it was no longer in its proper place, because the stars around it had changed their brightness and places. Then it was as though I was moving farther and farther away until I could not see the earth anymore. And the stars became more and more until there was much light all around me. Then I woke up and found myself at awe of what I had just seen. Because it was so real and vivid. I laid there for a long time wondering what this meant because I don't have dreams that I remember. After a while I did fall asleep again and had one more dream. This one was about my life as a grown man. That I was going to meet someone of which I could not see their face, but the rest of the image was clear and sharp. The person I saw is now my wife and my help meet. I know this because as I said, the rest of the image was very clear. Her hair and figure and also her hands could be seen and she was wearing a wedding dress. And she was at the New York baseball stadium. As you most likely have already guessed, she is from New York. After this I woke up again in total amazement. I could not understand all these things at that young age so I hid this in my heart and told no one and even forgot about the dreams until I meant her and came to know her for some time and then I remembered the dreams and told her about them. It was after this that the Lord began showing me the things that were to shortly come. Not as a vision, but by opening some of the prophecies in the book of Revelation. For you see, I still don't remember my dreams and I still can't close my eyes and see any images. But in the days while I was writing about the prophecies of the book of Revelation the Lord did give me a vision of the world to come. I could not see myself for it was like I was flying over fields and mountains and valleys. The colors were so deep and vivid that it was breathless. There are no words that I know to describe the beauty of what I saw, but I could <u>feel</u> the colors. What I have just told you is the most I have see in my life concerning dreams and the one vision that I have had. Because of this I have been jokingly saying to the Lord for a long time. Lord I am your blind servant. Well there really isn't much more to say about me. I'm a common man with no special talent or skill. It is the Lord and His Glory that this Testament is all about and my flesh profit nothing to it Do not judge this testament by reason of me, but by the words that are written here in. If the prophecies written in this testament do not come to pass. Then listen not to what it says and give it no place in you. For the words written here in shall be a testimony unto itself that it is the truth, even as He who spoke them is Truth. Even so Oh Lord, come .

Amen........

~ *The First Adam* ~
{remember}

Let me remember from within myself the place of my beginning. For it is there that I beheld perfection. For God was my beginning. He formed me and gave breath to me. That I might talk with him and he with me. That I might know him, even as he knows me. Should I return to this place in me, it is there that I may worship him. Both in spirit and in truth. If I worship him he will walk with me openly and I shall remember him in my beginnings. Should my blindness keep me from finding this place and I worship him not but only seek to do so, He will follow me and keep me in His way and I will find this place, because he wants me even as I want him. He is my Father and I am his son. For no man knowth the son, but the Father and likewise no man knowth the Father, but the son and he to whom he should reveal it unto. These words are of old and the echo remains. If it remains there is an ear to hear it. If it is heard, then it shall be forthcoming and accomplished. Who is the Father? First you must ask yourself. Who am I ? For there are the children, the godhead, the father of lies and God Almighty. And of course, God Almighty and Godhead they do know themselves. They know their own name. Even the evil one knows his own name and he is twice dead. God Almighty is Father of all things. Good and Evil, dead or alive. Godhead has Father, Son, Holy Spirit. The Father of all flesh is also the Father of Godhead, the first Adam. The second Adam, Christ became the Father, our Father. For so it seemed good in the Father's sight, to give all power and all authority unto the son. All things must be put under him, even the Father (Father of Godhead). So we have in the Godhead, the Father and the Son, who became the Father of all the children of the Resurrection and we have the Holy Spirit who is God Almighty of whom none have seen him not even the host of heaven, the Great <u>I am</u>. Yet Christ said that the Holy Spirit is his Father and that he knows him, that is to say his name. Therefore, in the word of Truth we have the Father mentioned in different context and it is needful to read it in that manner. Who you are will determine who your father is. The first Adam is the Father of your flesh and the second Adam, Christ is the Father of your new spirit. And he said that you could pray to Him or to His Father, the Holy Spirit, because they are One. And then there is the Father of Lies which is our old spirit by default. And as to the One who has become our Heavenly Father. To know Him, you must remember Him. Yet if you see Him you will surely remember Him. For He is the source to all things. And by the power of His name we are all made ' <u>Alive</u> '!...

Amen and Amen......

~ *Mystery Of The Great I Am* ~

He who <u>was</u> and <u>is</u> and who <u>will be</u> has said: "I am that I am". When He <u>was</u>, there was none who stood beside Him. And to this cause did He make Himself "Not" so that He might bring forth All things, even the Creation .

And because He <u>Is</u>, His name is All and All and the creation is the evidence of His Being. And His Will and His Works became the Holy Ghost who's power and Authority comes from the "Not", that is to say He who is in "Secret" . Because He speaks not His own, but that which He hears, which proceeds forth out of the mouth of God.

And because He is <u>yet to come</u>, He shall reveal Himself to all things He has created and there is nothing that will not see Him. For His Will is above all things and there is nothing that can deny Him. Not even the impossible things. The things of His pleasure shall receive great reward and glory, even Life Everlasting. And the things of His displeasure shall receive great wrath and torment, even to Everlasting pains of Death without end. For He is the God of Righteousness and He is making Holy all things which He has Made. Yet He is a God of order, therefore He has set something's to their nature and course so they would not change, but be perpetual. That is to say, the life supporting components. But the greater beings of life did He give Freedom of choice that they may chose their nature and course, even as He has done. To this cause they are called Sons of God. Of such are the Heavenly, and the Foul of Heaven, and the sons of Adam. Even so, He is all knowing and has prepared places for all things made, so that when the course is finished He shall Reveal Himself to His "Ancients Gloriously". And the Ark of His Testament shall be seen openly as a witness unto all and then all things shall be put in their places. And all rewards shall be given, both Good and Evil, even Great and small. And with them (Son of Man and His Children of the Resurrection) He shall Create a New and Everlasting Kingdom. And then He shall put on His Creation as a garment. And True Life shall be seen openly and at last begin. And the Waters of Life shall be given Freely and the True riches shall be found in the hands of the Living. For in the "Here and Now" God, that is to say the Invisible, Yet Omnipresent Holy Spirit, did make Himself "Not", so that All and All can be. For how else can there be Good and Evil. And why else would He let it be. For He has made All things for His Son and His Son, like Him has set them Free. And the Light of Their Glory is One. And the Children of Light shall we become, even an Host unto Their Glory. Even so Oh Lord, Let it be.

Amen and Amen......

~ *Mystery* Of The *Creation* Of God ~

Before the Heaven and the Earth there is "God" Because He always was, and is Life Inherent. For He is Eternity. Yet there was no one else beside Him. And He said: I shall bring forth a Son and He is our righteousness. Therefore I shall begin a work and it shall be non ending and therefore a part of Eternity with me, even the Creation of God. He is an Image and a likeness unto me. Therefore the works He has seen me doing, He shall do likewise. Because We are One and there is no division among Us.

So God Almighty said: "Let there be Light". And it was so. Then He created the Heaven and the Earth. Now in Heaven it was seen of the coming of the Son of God as a Mystery. Because the Son was with the Father from His beginning. For He the Son is the True Witness of God. Because He was with Him during the First Estate. For He stayed with the Father while the third of Heaven (First fruits) was cast down by the Great Red Dragon (known as the Devil, Satan, the Cherub that covereth, and the serpent). But in The First Estate Lucifer was his name, even the Son of the Morning. And he caused all things to come to Not. Then God and His Christ moved across the face of the waters because darkness was upon the face of the deep. And this was Our Beginning, even the "Here and Now". And God planted a garden east of Eden and put Adam there to keep it and dress it. And in the garden was the Tree of Life and the Tree of the Knowledge of Good and Evil. Then came Eve and to this cause when Eve stood before the Tree of the Knowledge of Good and Evil the serpent did speak with her. Therefore Satan was not in Heaven nor on the throne at this time, because of his deeds in the First Estate, which is the Knowledge of Good and Evil. To this cause was he bound unto this tree. Now when Eve ate of the fruit and gave unto Adam and he did eat, then Satan was released from the Tree, but the serpent was changed and made to eat from the dust of the ground which God had cursed. Then Satan in the passing of time ascended unto Heaven as he swore to God he would do and became the Accuser of the brethren. Then in the time appointed He the Son of God came down from God the Father unto us and was given the name "Emanuel" (God with us). For it is in the "Here and Now", Our Beginning that the Son came to start receiving the Life and Glory of His Kingdom (the First Fruits and their remnant),even the Nations. Now before the Son came upon the earth, that which was done in Heaven would manifest in part upon the earth. But in His coming He did command: That which is done on earth shall be done in heaven. To this cause He has given us this choice by reason of this commandment so that we might receive the desires of our heart, because of His Love for us. Because He is the purpose and cause of all good things done in the "Here and Now". For He Is the God of Heaven and Earth as the All Mighty has made Him to be. Even so Oh Lord.

Amen and Amen.......

~ *Our Beginning* ~

In The Beginning God created the heaven and the earth. This was "The First Estate". In the passing of time it came to <u>Not</u> because the Shinning One (The Cherub who covers) was found with iniquity in His Heart. This caused him to change the Light thereof. Because God gave him the light therefore he had the power to change it. To this cause is it written that He can change or transform Himself into an Angel of Light. When He changed the Light He changed Man also. To this end was it written: To replenish the earth and also the regeneration of son of man. For He knew of the things to come and that Man shall become the High Ones of the Kingdom. To this cause was it written: You desire the things of man rather then the things of God. And because He changed many things the Kingdom or Estate came to Not. Then came <u>Our Beginning</u> and the earth was without form and void; and darkness was upon the Face of the Deep. And the Spirit of God moved upon the Face of the Waters. And God said, *"Let there be Light"*. And there was Light. After all these things which God had done to fulfill the Light which He Made in the Beginning of Days. Then came Adam who was put in the Garden of Eden and a Tree of Life in the mist of the garden. And there was also a Tree of the Knowledge of Good and Evil. And a Serpent who was more subtle then all the beast of the field, which knew of the Tree of the Knowledge of Good and Evil and the power therein. Because <u>He</u> was not only the <u>keeper</u> of it, but also <u>bound</u> by it because of <u>His</u> <u>deeds</u> in the <u>knowledge</u> there of. It was and is <u>His Light</u> which <u>He</u> <u>Made</u>. And now God has chosen to change it for our sakes because He swore unto Himself, because there was none who stood beside Him. That His words would not come back to Him <u>Empty</u> and <u>Void</u>. Therefore Christ and those found in Him must come forth to fulfill that which was spoken by God Himself in The Beginning of Days when He said: "Let There Be Light". And it was so... And this I say also: God can do all things. This made Lucifer desire to make God do what He swore not to do. For you see if you say it, it must come to pass. God said He would never leave you or forsake you. To this end does the Evil One work in us continually to make God a liar to Himself and us. The only thing God can't do is what He said He wouldn't do.!!

Amen.......

Now when God said: It is not good that the Man should be alone. He caused Adam to go into a deep sleep and removed a rib from him to build Eve. This in turn divided Adam, but as long as <u>they</u> were <u>one</u> in God's order they were <u>whole</u>. But in the fall they became divided, because they were not one in God's order anymore, but rather in Satan's order for He had deceived Eve and Adam was willing to fall for her, because he was not deceived (1 Tim 2:14), but did love her because he said: This is now bone of my bones, and flesh of my flesh: She shall be called Woman, because she was taken out of a man. To this cause they fell from God and into Death which caused God to drive them out of the Garden where the Tree of Life is to this day. For had they taken from the Tree of Life while they are dead. Then they would remain that way for ever and ever and they would not want the salvation of Christ. Even as Satan does not want it. For Christ came to put Satan back in His Tree of The Knowledge of Good and Evil. And Man back to The Tree Of Life. This I tell you in truth, we the children of Adam are born in Death, because our Father was dead when he came to know Eve. And we are like him. Yet the promise of God's blessing is in him and Christ came as a man to fulfill it. And it was so. If the dead are to be made "Alive" there must be judgment, so that which is dead and that which is "alive "can be separated. For they are presently one flesh. For in death they were born and in death shall they be separated. For God has chosen to take that which is dead and make it alive. To this cause is there the Resurrection. One of "Righteousness" and One of "Damnation". For all things are "Alive" unto God.To this end has He chosen to make "Alive" whom he will through His Son that they should become Sons of God and enter-in unto Life being separated from Death. Living not by flesh and yet having body. For Christ has judged the flesh and saved His body for us-ward that we should be like him and He should take on our likeness. To this cause did He (The Word) become flesh to be tempted in all points and yet desire the things of God rather then the things of Men. That He should give All of Himself for us and to God that we could be reconciled back unto God in His Flesh which shall become our Body. I said reconciled because we came from Him in the light which was given unto the Shinning One in the Beginning of the First Estate of which he the Shinning One did change because of his heart. To this cause did the Lord speak of the 'Regeneration' of Son of Man. And in Genesis God said to 'Replenish' the earth. For this reason the Spirit of God moved across the face of the waters because there was Darkness upon the face of the deep. For in this Beginning God said "Let there be Light "And God saw the Light, that it was good. And God divided the Light from the Darkness. We are not talking about the stars and planets because they were called into existence on the fourth day . Not the first day. This Light that God said was good is His Word which He gave to One in the Beginning when He created the heaven and the earth. And this One He did receive it with gladness, but in the passing of time this One changed the Light and made it into Darkness. Yet God said: *My Words will not return to me Empty and Void*. So God divided The Light From The Darkness and the evening and the morning were the first day.This is only to bring out that which was covered or hidden from Our Beginning so that you might know what the mystery of the times and seasons concerning the universe, our world and the age of which we live. For our science tells us that the universe is rather old and the Bible tells us that by comparison the Earth is younger. The correct answer is:The Beginning {First Estate}. Our Beginning {The Here and Now} The division of Light and Darkness. We do not need this knowledge for salvation but to fulfill the words of the Lord. *There is nothing covered that shall not be revealed: and hid, that shall not be known.* Let me keep it simple so that we can apply it to the whole. How did the planets and the stars have their beginning? And what has a planet and the stars have in common with each other? The first question has several schools of thought concerning:creation,design intelligence or spontaneous expansion. But to explain how they formed is the issue here and not who or by what force began the process. Nevertheless, in their beginning came forth a great mass of molted hot matter in different sizes because of the force and intensity of the expansion. The space, which was also expanding, was very cold and the hot matter began to cool on its surface. As the matter cooled it began to contract, which caused the center of the mass or core to compress. This in turn caused neutrons to begin forming in the core or center of the mass because the atom's electrons were being collapsed into their nucleus. Now the larger the forming heavenly body is, then the longer the cooling process and also the larger that the forming neutron core would become. As this process increased, then gravity began to pull on the mass, which caused the elements within the mass to stir and mix and form different deposits as it was cooling inwardly. It is here at this moment that the planets and the stars share their commonality, which is the developing of gravity. The force of gravity will be determined by the size of the mass which is cooling. As it cools and compresses then the core begins to grow, which increases the gravity. The smaller masses started forming their gravity first, which was the planets. Now the cooling process is what caused the mass to compress, which caused the gravity to develop and this process, of course would be much slower for the larger masses, which formed the stars. As the larger masses cooled and the core becomes larger, then the increase of gravity will reach a point where the surface of the mass, even though it has cooled and hardened, would become molted again because of nuclear fusion. This being because of the intensity of the gravity by reason of the neutron core and its size. The size of the core will determine the movement of space around the mass or heavenly body as well as the stability of space in proportion to the circumference of the core, which will determine the area of space that becomes unstable once the core mass reaches energy threshold. This being the point where the mass of the heavenly body and the amount of space that this mass displaces becomes less then the amount of space the core mass collapses or draws-in because of its nature, which is two thirds greater then normal mass. This becomes the means of nuclear fusion. And the birth of a star. With this concept in mind consider this; The universe consist of three (3) components. Space, Matter, Anti-Matter. Space, which we have never understood or comprehended is the first one. We will call this one "the container". Then we have matter, which takes up space or displaces it.That is to say fill it up. Some say it has weight, but weight is a function of attraction that is determined by space not matter. The last is anti-matter, which collapses or draws-in the same amount of space that matter would fill up or displace. This is why it appears to have mass, but it does not. So matter has mass and takes up space and anti-matter has no mass and collapses space. The name of matter is Proton. The name of anti-matter is Electron. Now the Neutron is the coming together of the proton and the electron. This can happen if the two are traveling at high speeds and at a collision course. Should this happen then you have the Neutron, which takes on the character of both matter and anti-matter. It causes space to be "displaced" then "collapsed" at the speed of light. The present belief is that if matter and anti-matter should come together it would cause a great explosion. What it really causes is this thing we call <u>Gravity</u>. When you get enough neutrons together it will move space in such a way that matter is drawn to it, because space is reacting to the double effect of the neutrons and everything in that area of space must and will be affected by reason of it. I should also mention that the reason why matter and anti-matter don't generally collide is because one turns or spins clockwise and the other counter clockwise. Kind of like the weather conditions of high and low pressures and the directions they move. And while spinning the space around them creates like a bubble or envelope that turns in the same direction. This cushion is why they never touch unless moving at a high speed. This is also why they have an electrical charge which is different then a gravity field. The electrical charge is actually the reaction of space that these two components cause which are opposites and we see that as its charge, which holds the atoms and molecules together. And of course the gravitational one holds the Heavenly bodies in Place. All of this is so that life can exist. Today it is believed that the electrical force is the greater one. It is not so! The electrical force can not be increased which holds the atoms together. It is what it is and can not be changed. If you could stack matter together until it was the size of our sun, you could not produce a gravitational field and the electrical field would not increase by reason of the size of this matter and to this cause the electrical field is the weaker of the two forces that exist in the universe. And gravity the greater. Now space the "container" of matter can be comprehended by thinking of it as a liquid. But first you need to understand a different concept of solid and liquid substances. We look at matter the wrong way. We say matter is either solid, liquid or gas. And this is true, but if you look at something solid you must realize it is not, but rather it has a lot of space within it. And if you look at something liquid you must realize it is more solid, because it has little space within it. And of course if you look at something in the form of gas you will find even more space then you find in that which you call solid. Now that we have this concept before us, consider this: Space is like the opposite of liquid in the same way that matter and anti-matter are opposites of each other. As we spoke of it earlier. One having mass and the other appearing to have mass, but not. So space will flow in a manner like unto liquid where there is matter or anti-matter to affect it. And this is the so called lines of force we call Gravity and Magnetic fields. Where there is no matter or very little matter, space will have little or no measurable gravity. Making the space like still waters. But where there is much matter, space will move according to the density of the matter that it contains. It is this movement that causes the atoms to move in the order that they do. And why certain elements can have its atoms (molecules) to align in such a way that it produces a magnetic field. The orbit of the electrons around the nucleus and the effect that electrons have on space, that is to say to gather space and the envelop that is produced holds the nucleus together, and the space in the immediate area is stable and flowing, and under the right conditions the electrons will share orbits with the adjacent atoms and molecules which will align the atoms in such a way that the electrons will cause the space to turn in a circular motion which creates the lines of force called a magnetic field. If you have current flow through a wire (electron flow) it will produce a small magnetic field. If you coil the wire then the field will become stronger because of the circular motion of the electrons in a given area of space. The strength of the field is determined by the mass and the amount of current flowing in the matter and how much of a curve that the surface of the matter has. If to much current is applied the nucleus will expand causing heat to be generated, which will cause the atoms to disperse and the magnetic field will cease to exist and the matter will change or be converted to light or heat energy. To this cause you are limited to the size and strength of a magnetic field. Which is created by reason of the electrons and its effect on space and the quantity there of which is also limited to the density of the matter. The more dense the matter the more current or lines of force needed to produce the field. Which again limits how large the field will be and its strength. I should also mention that the sharing of electrons causes space to flow in the alignment of the nucleus (positive) and electrons (negative) of the matter which creates the poles of the field. For space will flow in the direction of positive to negative. In this same manner space reacts to neutrons with the exception that there is no alignment in a neutron core such as a Neutron Star or Black Hole. For the gravitational lines of force are without negative and positive poles. Unless there is matter orbiting close enough around it to create the poles by reason of its mass. Where as to a planet or sun, the gravitational lines of force, that is to say lines of space are passing through stable matter and space causing a flow from its nucleus which will make it flow from positive to negative thereby creating gravitational poles and of course the push pull effect of the core is what creates the lines of force of gravity which appears similar to magnetic fields because it is space and its movement that is common between the two (2) forces as well as the effect electrons and neutrons have as space reacts to them. Now electromagnetic fields are as magnetic fields, because one is created by forcing electron flow in the matter and the other is by natural alignment of the molecules of said matter by reason of the type of elements that it consist of. As I had said earlier. For this reason it has been thought for many decades that electromagnetic and magnetic fields were similar, but not the same forces. But as I said they are the same, just created differently. One being temporary (while current is flowing) and the other more permanent by reason of nature. Now gravitational force can be increased by reason of the size of the heavenly body. Therefore, the more neutrons you have together as a core, the greater the force. The size of the core is always proportional to the size of the heavenly body. If the size of the body is large enough then the core size will generate a strong enough force to break down the matter on its surface and you will get what is called nuclear fusion. This being a sun or star by reason of its size. The other thing I should mention is because of the nature of what we call matter is, there is a lot of space in atoms and molecules. Such space is at a stable state if the matter is stable. If the matter is unstable so is the space. Now the neutron core troubles space because of its nature, which is kind of like a push pull effect. And the mass around the core will help stabilize the space to a point. But if the core is large enough then the distance of space, which is determined by the circumference of the core will start breaking down to the very surface of the matter and the space will become greatly troubled and the matter will become unstable and fusion will occur. Once the fusion begins and the matter is breaking down on the surface then the core will begin to increase in size at a slow rate, which causes the area of troubled space to increase in both directions. That is to say inward and outward. It is by reason of this process a sun would nova and implode or invert into a black hole. This will depend on the size of the heavenly body and of course the type of material it consist of. If the sun is small enough in size when most of the mass is consumed it will cause the remaining mass, if dense enough to expand to the size of the troubled field for a short period and then it will collapse. This causing an implosion, which disperses the core and you will most of the time end up with a cloud remaining. If the core is large enough to adsorb the implosion, then you will have what is called a dark star. You can detect the gravity field, but you can't see a star. If it is large enough it will be seen by the amount of matter that is drawn to it as it is growing. This of course will become so large that nothing will be able to disperse it. Even if a large heavenly body should collide with it. This is the fate of the universe, which has its number of days. With this in mind consider this: The Earth was without form and void; and darkness was upon the face of the deep. This was the state before our beginning and will also be at our end. But then God said *"let there be light"* : and there was light. So let not your heart be troubled concerning the fate of this universe. Because this is our first home not our last one. We are not meant to remain here to be consumed in the manner as it is written concerning the Heavens: *And the heaven departed as a scroll when it is rolled together. And again; But the day of the lord will come as a thief in the night; in the which the heavens shall pass away with a great noise, and the elements shall melt with fervent heat, the earth also and the works that are therein shall be burned up.* Yet before this event comes there is a calamity that comes first: *The earth shall reel to and fro like a drunkard, and shall be removed like a cottage; and the transgression thereof shall be heavy upon it; and it shall fall, and not rise again. And it shall come to pass in that day, that the Lord shall punish the <u>Host</u> of the <u>High Ones</u> that are on high, and the <u>Kings</u> of the earth <u>upon</u> the <u>earth</u>. And they shall be <u>gathered</u> together, as <u>prisoners</u> are gathered in the pit, and shall be shut up in the prison, and after <u>many days</u> shall they be <u>visited</u>.* The time spoken of here is the time of the Rapture, which begins the time of the Two Witnesses. But before this comes to pass the Lord must have His Angels accomplish that which He spoke of in His generation when He the Lord said that He would go from one end of heaven to the other gathering His Children. He has been doing so for almost two thousand years. His Angels have been gathering the Nations by their deeds which are governed by their Hearts. Look at their laws and the things they call good.God gave His Fruitfulness to the Gentiles that He should display His ability to control our History. For we must fulfill His Words. If we are His children we will hear His voice and perform His will even though we may not know what that will is. If the Lord should reveal it unto you it is your reward to rejoice in it with Him. What are the desires of your heart? The Lord deals with us not only as a people (Nation), but as individuals. Knowing us by name. Is it not written He searches the Hearts and reins of men? He will give to each of His children according to their treasures. You and I can't see what's in a man's heart for there is more to life then the body. How then shall we judge what we can't see ? We must give this judgment to this One who is in Secret. The same will reveal the things that are and the things that do appear. To this cause we should witness only. As to the things that appear: There are many who will say we wait for the thousand years of peace for the Lord will reign on the earth with us. The Lord Himself said this is not His Kingdom. He also said: *Think not that I am come to send peace on the earth: I came not to send peace, but a sword.* The time we are presently living is the Second Death. For the First Resurrection ended when Satan was released which is when there was an increase of knowledge. As it is written in Daniel: *many shall run to and fro, and knowledge shall be increased.* For he uses Knowledge to deceive the Nations. As it is written: *there is a way that seems right unto a man, but the end there of leads unto destruction.* This is the means which he destroys wonderfully. Know this, knowledge without wisdom brings much sorrows. Even unto desolation. To this cause the Evil One has opened our minds to earthly knowledge that we should be overwhelmed and withdrawn from truth. That we should go all in our own way. Seeing ourselves as wise thinking our knowledge has wisdom within it. Knowledge in its self is not good or evil, but what you do with it. This is where wisdom should come in. Without the use of wisdom your knowledge will cause more harm then good. Even our history has proven this to be true. In medicine, machinery, agriculture and government, just to name a few of them. As I said, the evil one has used this knowledge to confuse us in its grandness and we stand in awe of it. In our present state we are using our knowledge mostly for evil and little for good . Thanks be to God that He is with us because without Him we can do no good at all. I say these things not to change what we are doing, because Evil must have its day. But to make it known that we are in the Second Death and all these things must come to pass and that these things make it self evident of the time and season we live in. For many believe that we will have a thousand years of peace in the First Resurrection and therefore this present time can not be the Second Death. But I tell you a Truth, the Lord Himself said He came not with peace, but a sword and that this is not His Kingdom, but He came to receive unto Himself that which the Father gave Him. And also this, that He will return again to receive <u>all</u> that which is <u>His</u> so that <u>they</u> should be where <u>He</u> is also, which is <u>His Kingdom</u>. Consider this, if He were to setup a Kingdom here in this world, then why would it last only a thousand years and then end? Because His Kingdom will last forever and ever and have no end. Do you not yet understand? This Kingdom belongs to another and it will remain his forever. And all that remains shall be cast into the Lake of Fire. Yea, Death and Hell shall be emptied into the Lake of Fire and even heaven and earth shall no longer be found and yet the smoke of it shall forever and ever ascend up unto God. This is the fate of this kingdom and He to whom it belongs. Therefore, believe the Gospel and repent and eat the flesh of the Holy One and drink His Blood that you may be <u>made worthy</u> to stand with Him in this time of choice, which shall end after the time of the Two Witnesses is fulfilled. Be not among those who shall become angry when His Wrath has come! Remember this: There are those who are from the First Resurrection and the Second Death has no power over them. The same shall help us and a great multitude will enter into life from the Second Death. For the First fruits were many, but the great multitudes come out of the Second Death. The First Resurrection is for the First fruits onto God and His Christ. For the Lord said His Father gave them to Him that He the Lord should glorify the Father in them. For the Lord rose up early and sent the law and the prophets. He sent the law as a guide line to teach us. Not to destroy us because of our weakness. For He is made strong in our weakness. And He sent the prophets to reveal the things that are hidden or covered up from Our Beginning. Not that we need it to have life more Abundantly, but because He said all things must be revealed that was hidden from Our Beginning. Then the end of Death can come. For God promised to His Prophets that they would understand in time why things happened the way they have. The Lord said: *Had I not come and did what none other man did. You have not sinned.* Therefore, had He not come then we would not have a need for salvation. For then we would have had a <u>Cloak</u> for our <u>sin</u>. Even as this One had a Cloak for sin, but now it is <u>removed</u>. To this cause did Christ come. Now <u>we must believe</u> in <u>Him</u> as well as <u>call on His Name</u> that He should work in us. For if we will eat His flesh (learn of Him) and drink His blood (learn His doctrine and walk in it). He will be faithful and forgive us and heal us of our infirmities. For even the Devil believes in Christ. But he does not believe in His ways. Because the Lord said the Father is Greater then I. And Satan said that He was equal to God. This means that Satan believes in Himself more then anything else. If that hits a soft spot, then you might want to turn around and take a long look at yourself to see what's in your eye. Consider, What is Truth? This question has been asked from our beginning. When the Serpent said to Eve; Genesis 3:1, *And he said unto the woman, Yea, hath God said, Ye shall not eat of every tree of the garden?* And also Genesis 3:4 *And the serpent said unto the woman, Ye shall not surely die*: For you see Evil came before mankind (Eve) and asked the question, What is Truth? Then suggested that the Truth was actually a Lie and made the statement that the Lie was actually the truth. Even saying it will cause confusion to you. From that day to this, has the question remained. Many have come and said, this is Truth and will lead all who will hear them to a deeper place which will not answer the question; What is Truth? The answer can be found in a little book that was given to John, of which he did eat, and it was bitter-sweet. Because it was sweet to the mouth and yet bitter to the belly. Sweet to the mouth because as he ate it (understood the Mystery) he began to know the Love of God for Man and the fulfillment of His Promises to us in the Spirit. Yet, in knowing this he also came to know the things that must follow and manifest unto the body and therefore mankind, even to the end time. This was bitter to the belly or body because of the things man must suffer to fulfill the Words of God, because of One who hid the Truth and made a Lie to stand. For the brethren, that is to say, fellow-servants must walk in the Second Death and not only witness the three Woes, but also be part of the revealing. And this is Truth: There is Good and there is Evil. God has made all that is found within this statement. That which is evil, shall seek to itself. And likewise, that which is good, shall seek to itself. This is God actively fulfilling His Words. And when He is finished He shall put all that is Evil in one place and all that is Good in another. To this cause should we make the tree Good or make the tree Evil. It is a choice we need to make for ourselves, because God wants us to have that which we desire. Therefore, be not deceived, because there is One who desires for you to believe that you want to be like "him" and not like the Lord. For he will display love, kindness, concern for others and peace, but only if he can profit by reason of these acts. There is no Love of Heart found here. There is only love of possession and love of self glory. To this cause there is no mercy or compassion found in him. For you see, he is the one who said; do these good works to those who need it and both you and them can profit by it and that is good. And I say unto you; where is it written that the Lord said to make profit on the things you do for those who need help? This One will also say to you; God wants you to prosper and therefore make profit. And I would say; God shall bring His blessings unto you and you shall increase by reason of it. He will not have <u>you make</u> His increase unto you. Even though He will bless the works of your hands, but that is to increase or magnify your works, not His. Therefore know what is Truth and choose of whom you shall be for ever and ever and take on that likeness. For God shall in <u>His time</u>, which is soon, seal us all unto our place. And it shall surly be done. Evil shall resist this work and Good shall yield to it. If you are a part of the Good, then God shall draw you to Him and His Words shall strengthen you and comfort you. And His ways shall become your ways and you will take on His likeness. Slow to anger and quick to forgive and always willing to help those who call on the Name of the Lord. When God created all things in the Beginning, this was the nature of all things made. Even the Shinning One, Son of the Morning. But in the passing of time his beauty caused him to corrupt his wisdom and he no longer wanted to be a likeness unto God, but wanted to be equal to Him and then become Him in All things by reason of his Equality. Thereby being above All things, even the Father of Creation. It was this desire that gave birth to the Lie and the Beginning of the Father of Lies. For it was in that day that <u>Iniquity</u> was <u>found</u> in his <u>Heart</u>. And also in that day that he transformed the Light of God into his light, which is Darkness, even the tree of the Knowledge of Good and Evil. And the Kingdom (The First Estate) came to Not and Darkness was upon the face of the Deep. And to this cause did the Old Serpent deceive Eve in Our Beginning, so that what God is Doing to fulfill His Light in the <u>Here</u> and <u>Now</u> the Evil One is resisting by making us blind with his Light, even a Knowledge so that we should follow him and not hear what is Truth unto Life Everlasting. For Life Everlasting requires "Trust of God", which is Faith in the Son Of God and His Works and calling on His Name. And <u>trust</u> in the <u>Knowledge</u> of the <u>world</u> will <u>lead</u> you into <u>Darkness</u> and the <u>deception</u> thereof, which comes from the Evil One. As you know, Knowledge has power and the greater the Knowledge, then the greater the power. By this reasoning know that he comes with a great Knowledge and power to persuade you into believing him. That you should trust him by reason of his strength. For to trust in Knowledge of this world, that is to say universe. You are also saying trust in the God of the earth with your eternal life. And if you put your trust in the God of Heaven and earth. He shall be your reward. Even so Oh Lord let us receive of You.

Amen........

Consider this, Great Light and Great Darkness look the same outwardly, but not inwardly. For with Great Light you can see endlessly. And with Great Darkness you can only see a far off. Because one has an end and the other does not. If the Lord heals us of our infirmities, we will have remembrance of Him. For He was our Real Father. For it was in <u>The Beginning</u> we were not allowed in Him, because of the Change {Lucifer}. But in Our Beginning a way was made that we can be grafted back in. For it was Lucifer who changed the Light and God who made it. And God who fulfilled it. Because He said it was His Works and they are non ending, just as He is. That makes His Works Perfect, just like He is. The Works need Him, but He does not need the works. Because His Works are done in His Grace, which is His Love for us. For the Resurrection makes us the Children of the Resurrection, which makes us <u>as</u> the <u>Angels</u> of <u>God</u>, which brings us back into the Light where we should be. For in doing this we are then reconciled back to God. And all things are then restored that was lost in the First Estate, when the Great Red Dragon drew a third part of Heaven and did cast them unto the ground and did trodden them under his foot. Then in the passing of time did all things come to <u>not</u>; And the earth was without form, and void; and darkness was upon the face of the deep. And the Spirit of God moved upon the face of the waters. And this became Our Beginning. For God said in Our Beginning to be fruitful and multiply and replenish the earth. And in doing this shall He recover <u>all</u> that was lost. Then shall the End come and the Everlasting Begin. And to those who say; how can this be true? And why is this not written in the Bible? And this I say to you: The Lord said that the scribes of the Kingdom shall be as an <u>householder</u> who will bring out of his house <u>Old</u> and <u>New</u> things. It was by this means that the Lord spoke to the Prophets concerning the things hidden of Ancient Times. Such as it is written in Daniel: *One like the Son of man came with the clouds of heaven, and came to the "Ancient of days", and they brought Him near before Him.* For Ancient Of Days referrers to the First Estate. Like also what is written in Isaiah: *How art thou fallen from heaven "O Lucifer Son of the Morning".* And also this: *Then the moon shall be confounded, and the sun ashamed, when the Lord of hosts shall reign in mount Zion, and in Jerusalem, and before his "<u>Ancients</u>" gloriously.* And also in Ezekiel : *Thou art the Anointed Cherub that covereth ; and I hath set thee so: thou wast upon the Holy Mountain of God; thou hast walked up and down in the mist of the "Stones of Fire".* In the time of the prophets these things were new and yet of old. Yes, these things were hidden from the time of Our Beginning. And likewise in the last days, shall more things of old be shown as new. For how else shall the hidden things come forth. And how shall we know what is true and what is false? For the things that are foretold to come to pass is the measuring that we should use and how we can tell from whom the report has come. To this cause the Lord has given us signs of the time and season. That we should hear Him when He speaks. And to whom he speaks through, as it is written: *For with stammering lips and another tongue will He speak to this people.* For in this Testament are things written that must surely come to pass. Because He reveals unto His Children that which must surly come. To this cause do I say, all these things must come to pass. And if not, then hear not the words of this Testament and give not place in you for it. But <u>He</u> who <u>gave</u> them to <u>me</u> said: Write these words in a book of testament and make them a witness to the people that the time is at hand that I will perform and accomplish the words therein. And the <u>words given</u> you <u>before</u> <u>hand</u> put also in this book and bear witness of it to them that they shall know that I have been with you, even though you are just a man. For I remember you and have brought you to this place for this cause.

    Therefore I, even I a man such as yourself do here bear witness that as I have <u>chosen</u> to <u>believe</u> what I have <u>seen</u> and <u>heard</u> and have <u>written</u> in this <u>Testament</u> as a <u>witness</u> unto all. That they who read these words may choose also. Even so Oh Lord, come quickly.

Amen and Amen.....

~ *Parable* ~

Matt. 25:1 *Then shall the <u>kingdom</u> of <u>heaven</u> be <u>likened</u> unto ten virgins, which took their lamps, and went forth to meet the bridegroom. 2 And five of them were wise, and five were foolish. 3 They that were foolish took their lamps, and took no oil with them: 4 But the wise took oil in their vessels with their lamps. 5 While the bridegroom tarried, they all slumbered and slept. 6 And at midnight there was a cry made, Behold, the bridegroom cometh; go ye out to meet him. 7 Then all those virgins arose, and trimmed their lamps. 8 And the foolish said unto the wise, Give us of your oil; for our lamps are gone out. 9 But the wise answered, saying, Not so; lest there be not enough for us and you: but go ye rather to them that sell, and buy for yourselves. 10 And while they went to buy, the bridegroom came; and <u>they that were ready</u> went in with him to the marriage: and the door was shut. 11 Afterward came also the other virgins, saying, Lord, Lord, open to us. 12 But he answered and said, Verily I say unto you, I know you not...·*

The meaning is this: The 10 virgins are the house of God, which has been divided into a house of five. As it is written in Matt. 9:52 For *<u>from henceforth</u> there shall be <u>five in one</u> <u>house</u> divided, three against two, and two against three.* The five wise virgins are those who <u>understood </u>the time and season and prepared themselves and brought oil in their vessels, which is the <u>anointing</u> so that while they waited for the call of the Bridegroom they would be ready for Him, because that which we need concerning Him the same He will provide for us, because He is our provider and He desires us to rely on Him, but we must <u>listen</u> for <u>His</u> <u>calling</u> and then we will always be ready. For the five wise virgins did enter and did partake of the marriage supper of the Lamb. For the <u>anointing</u> was with them, because it was their <u>time given</u>. And the other five virgins took their lamps, but did not get any oil nor did they prepare themselves and therefore <u>their time was not yet come</u>. For this cause when they returned and said Lord, Lord, open to us. He said, verily I say unto you, <u>I know you not</u>. The first five virgins was the house of God unto the First Resurrection. And the last five virgins are the house of God unto the Second Resurrection. And they shall know of the time and season of the Rapture and they shall enter in because <u>it is their time</u>. For the house of God is Glorified in both the First and the Second Resurrection and the fruit thereof. Now as to this house divided three against two and two against three. In the First Resurrection it was {Father, Son, Holy Spirit} the <u>God Head</u> against the <u>Beast</u> and the <u>False Prophet</u>. This saying that in the Lord's coming it was His time and He would over come the world (the Beast and the False Prophet). *Not by power, nor by strength, but by my Spirit,* saith the Lord. Now in the Second Resurrection the two against three are the <u>Beast</u> and the <u>Image</u> of the beast against the <u>God Head</u>.{Father, Son, Holy Spirit}. For he the Evil One must have His day and His time. And the fruit thereof. And He shall have it. Yet God shall be Glorified in this time also, even Magnified. Because out of the Great Tribulations come a great multitude. As it is written in Revelation: 7:9

> *9 After this I beheld, and, lo, <u>a great multitude, which no man could number, of all nations</u>, and <u>kindreds</u>, and <u>people</u>, and <u>tongues</u>, stood before the throne, and before the Lamb, clothed with white robes, and palms in their hands; And again, Rev. 7:13 And one of the elders answered, saying unto me, What are these which are arrayed in white robes? and whence came they? 14 And I said unto him, Sir, thou knowest. And he said to me, <u>These are they which came out of great tribulation</u>, and have washed their robes, and made them white in the blood of the Lamb.*

This magnification being a multitude which no man can number. Nevertheless, if we hear what the Spirit of Truth is speaking in this day, we will know the time and season and enter into the Rapture or be alive and remain to witness the strange work and the strange act which the Lord shall perform in the time of the Two Witnesses. For it is the will of the Heavenly Father that not one of these Little Ones should perish. Therefore many of those who go through great tribulation and are last to be received are also of old and first to be called, yet many were made unable to believe because of deception, not of the Truth, but of the time which they were called. And the time has come again unto them and they shall remember and they will hear without unbelief as the Two Witnesses give their Testimony. For the last shall be first and the first last. And how shall we know that this time and this season has really come unto us? Because it has been said before and yet it was not openly seen. In the last one hundred years man has seen more things come into existence then he has seen in the last six thousand years. Do you really think that we have become so much more intelligent in the last one hundred years? What did we eat or drink to account for this great increase in our brain power that we should just leap forward after thousands of years of being almost unchanged in our intellect. Yes, I know our technology is part of the reason for our jump ahead, but even technology needs intellect to grow. The answer to this question is <u>Inspiration</u>. We were made to be inspired. God has put it in our being that we should be inspired by Him and this is our perfection. But He has hidden His face from us and our nature will cause us to be inspired by <u>another</u> and to this cause we have become foolish in the science that we behold as God. Because this is where we go for understanding when we should be going to God. For if we seek <u>Him</u>, <u>He</u> will come to our awareness and <u>enlighten</u> us. Are we not His Children? And if we are His Children He will draw us unto Himself and we will not only want Him, but also seek Him, even if we hear unbelief within ourselves because of the Great Accuser. Because this is his time given him and he has used it to that cause, but the Lord said our time is always. So let not your heart be troubled nor your ear become dull of hearing or your Heart become hardened because the Evil One desires to have you and will use your weakness against you. Therefore use your strength against him. And what is your strength and how do you use it against him ? Trusting in the Lord is your strength. And staying in His word is how you use it, because the Holy Spirit will lead you as to what to say and what to do. For the Comforter is with us and He is speaking in this the Last Days. Even so Oh Lord.

Amen and Amen.....

Therefore, let not this One use your weakness against you. That is to say, blind you with great knowledge and false doctrine. For He can destroy you wondrously in His Strength, which is His Darkness..........

And yet how Great is that Darkness?.....

Is it not written that the Light pierced the Darkness and the Darkness comprehended it not? Therefore have trust in the word of God and know He will keep you in His way with His Spirit. And there is no power on earth or under the earth that can take you out of His Hand. Therefore stay in His Word and believe on Him and wait on His promises and His comforting. Consider Romans 15:4

For whatever things were written aforetime were written for our learning that we through <u>patience</u> and <u>comfort</u> of the <u>Scriptures</u> might have <u>hope</u>.

Amen and Amen.......

Now as to and concerning the Resurrection, of which there are two. One of Righteousness and one of Damnation ; It is needful to understand the meaning of the words which the Lord spoke when He said; *"I am the Resurrection"*. He also said ; *I am from above and you are from below.* The meaning is this: God The Father sent His Son into the world so that we might believe on Him by reason of the measure of faith which has been given to every man (Rom.12:3). All men who will believe on Him and try to walk in His ways shall be found in Christ.And if you are found in Christ then He has called you into His Resurrection. For you see if you are born again in spirit by believing on the Son of God, then you have entered into His Resurrection of life. And you have come out of the Resurrection of Damnation, which is what you were born into.You also must understand that while you are in this world which is full of Evil. You will stumble and sometimes fall, but in believing on the Lord you will always be picked up and will continue in His ways because the Holy Spirit will always be there to see to it that you will remain in the Lord's ways. Slow to anger and willing to forgive others even if they hurt you. To this cause the Lord also said ; *I am the Truth and the Life. Any man who will believe in me shall not die, but shall have Life Everlasting.* So you see, you will go from death to life in the moment you receive Him in Faith.And He will keep you in Himself by reason of the Holy Spirit. And here is where the saying is true; you shall pass from death to life.Because the Lord is from above and was sent from the Father and became flesh, even as we are. As it is written in Daniel 2:22 concerning the Father: *He revealeth the deep and secret things: he knoweth what is in the darkness, and the <u>Light</u> dwelleth with him.* The Light being Christ the Lord (The Word). And the Word became flesh.

Now He being found in the flesh was then tempted even as we are, but He knowing the Father then gave His flesh for us that we might believe on Him the Only Begotten of the Father. For He is like the Father and we are not. Yet if we can believe on Him and therefore become like Him, then we can also know the Father. For in believing in the Son we are given the power to become Sons of God, even as He is. It was the Father who gave the Son Life Inherent, which means He could lay His life down and pick it up again, Himself. And He has promised to do the same for us if we can believe on Him. This is why He said: *I am the Resurrection*. For the Father made all things for the Son and gave Him all Power and all Authority because He is also Son of Man. And His cause is to raise up as many as will <u>hear</u> Him. And make them as He is, that is to say Sons of God and they shall be like Him. To have Life Inherent and know the Father, that is to say His Name. As it is written in Rev.3:12; *Him that overcometh will I make a pillar in the <u>temple</u> of my God, and he shall go no more out: and I <u>will write</u> upon him the <u>name</u> of my God, and the name of the city of my God, which is <u>new</u> Jerusalem, which cometh down out of heaven from my God: and I will write upon him my <u>new</u> name.* Therefore if we will believe in Him and walk in His ways He will forgive us of our sins (that is to say when we stumble and fall because of the Evil One). We must remember that we not only have to believe the Lord is the Only Begotten of God, but also that He will keep us in Him by reason of the Holy Spirit. Then shall we be One in the Son, even as He is One in the Father. Then shall the Resurrection be complete and all things can be Made New. To this cause the Lord returns to receive All who believe in Him. And then the end of the Resurrection of Damnation shall come. And All that are on the earth in that day will see the Wrath of God Almighty. And the Great White Throne Judgment is come. And then the Beginning of the Everlasting Kingdom shall take on form and this is the BRIGHTNESS OF HIS COMING, even the GREAT I AM. And the Son's Light, even the " Bright and Morning Star " shall fill the New Heaven. And all that are found in Him shall be made to Shine as the Lights of Heaven. And we shall all know His " New Name". And shall be One in Him, even as He is in the Father. Even so Oh Lord come.

Amen and Amen........

~ Kingdoms ~

Daniel 2:31: *31 Thou, O king, sawest, and behold a great image. This great image, whose brightness was excellent, stood before thee; and the form thereof was terrible. 32 This image's head was of fine gold, his breast and his arms of silver, his belly and his thighs of brass, 33 His legs of iron, his feet part of iron and part of clay. 34 Thou sawest till that a stone was cut out without hands, which smote the image upon his feet that were of iron and clay, and brake them to pieces. 35 Then was the iron, the clay, the brass, the silver, and the gold, broken to pieces together, and became like the chaff of the summer threshing floors; and the wind carried them away, that no place was found for them:and the stone that smote the image became a great mountain, and filled the whole earth 36 This is the dream; and we will tell the interpretation thereof before the king. 37 Thou, O king, art a king of kings: for the God of heaven hath given thee a kingdom, power, and strength,and glory. 38 And wheresoever the children of men dwell, the beasts of the field and the fowls of the heaven hath he given into thine hand, and hath made thee ruler over them all. Thou art this head of gold.39 And after thee shall arise another kingdom inferior to thee, and another third kingdom of brass, which shall bear rule over all the earth. 40 And the fourth kingdom shall be strong as iron: forasmuch as iron breaketh in pieces and subdueth all things: and as iron that breaketh all these, shall it break in pieces and bruise. 41 And whereas thou sawest the feet and toes, part of potters' clay, and part of iron, the kingdom shall be divided; but there shall be in it of the strength of the iron, forasmuch as thou sawest the iron mixed with miry clay. 42 And as the toes of the feet were part of iron, and part of clay, so the kingdom shall be partly strong, and partly broken. 43 And whereas thou sawest iron mixed with miry clay, they shall mingle themselves with the seed of men: but they shall not cleave one to another, even as iron is not mixed with clay. 44 And in the days of these kings shall the God of heaven set up a kingdom, which shall never be destroyed: and the kingdom shall not be left to other people, but it shall break in pieces and consume all these kingdoms, and it shall stand for ever. 45 Forasmuch as thou sawest that the stone was cut out of the mountain without hands, and that it brake in pieces the iron, the brass, the clay, the silver, and the gold; the great God hath made known to the king what shall come to pass hereafter: and the dream is certain, and the interpretation thereof sure.*

This speaks of all the kingdoms of greatness that should come upon the earth, even to the end time. For which are of seven, even the eighth, which is of the seven. Consider Rev. 17:10

> *10 And there are seven kings: five are fallen, and one is, and the other is not yet come; and when he cometh, he must continue a short space. 11 And the beast that was, and is not, even he is the eighth, and is of the seven, and goeth into perdition.*

I tell you a Truth, the Kingdom which exist today is that Kingdom that must <u>continue</u> for a <u>short space</u>. For the five Kingdoms spoken of in Daniel 2:45 are the five Kingdoms which are spoken of in Rev. 17:10, (five are fallen). And the Kingdom in the time of our Lord Christ, was the sixth (and one is), even the one which had a deadly wound that healed. Rev. 13:3

3 And I saw one of his heads as it were wounded to death; and his deadly wound was healed: and all the world wondered after the beast. And this Beast is described in Rev. 13:1

13: 1 And I stood upon the sand of the sea, and saw a beast rise up out of the sea, having <u>seven heads</u> and ten horns, and upon his horns ten crowns, and <u>upon his</u> "heads" <u>the name of blasphemy</u>.

These seven heads are the seven Kings spoken of and their Kingdoms, because every Kingdom shall have a King. Now you should ask; Daniel spoke of five Kingdoms not seven! Yes He did, but he also said; in the days of these Kings, shall the God of heaven set up a Kingdom that shall never be destroyed. This work began in the sixth kingdom. Now this deadly wound of the sixth head came from Christ, because it was the time of the fulfillment of God's prophecy of the seed of the woman bruising the head of the seed of the serpent, Genesis 3: 15

3:15 And I will put enmity between thee and the woman, and between <u>thy</u> <u>seed</u> and <u>her</u> <u>seed</u>; it shall <u>bruise</u> thy <u>head</u>, and thou shalt <u>bruise</u> his <u>heel</u>.

The bruise became a deadly wound because the serpent chose to not bruise the heel of the seed of the woman (Christ), but rather to kill Him. And to this cause as he had done so was it done unto him. Consider the parable in Luke 20:9 and remember that in this parable there was one sent three times concerning the receiving of the fruits and then the son was sent. Nevertheless, these are the things of old and shall be fulfilled in the revealing of this man of sin, but as I was saying he chose to kill him. And he did receive a deadly wound of the head. And to this cause is it written in 1 Cor. 2:7

2: 7 But we speak the <u>wisdom</u> of <u>God</u> in a <u>mystery</u>, even the <u>hidden wisdom</u>, which God <u>ordained before</u> the <u>world</u> <u>unto</u> <u>our</u> <u>glory</u>: 8 Which none of the <u>princes</u> of this <u>world</u> knew: <u>for had they known it</u>, they would not have <u>crucified</u> the <u>Lord of glory</u>.

For this is that part which the Lord spoke of when He said in Matt.9:13

13 But go ye and learn what that meaneth, I will have <u>mercy</u>, and <u>not</u> <u>sacrifice</u>: for I am not come to call the righteous, but sinners to repentance. And again in Matt. 12: 7 But <u>if ye</u> had <u>known</u> <u>what this meaneth</u>, I will have <u>mercy</u>, and <u>not sacrifice</u>, ye would not have <u>condemned</u> the <u>guiltless</u>.

For the Lord came that He should take All sin away from All who would receive Him, because He said He would turn "None" away who would call on His Name or receive Him.. For I tell you a Truth, when the Lord spoke these words He was speaking unto the High Ones who heard Him not, in that day. For had they heard Him, then He would not have sacrificed. To this cause is it written in John 18: 3-9

3 Judas then, having received a band of men and officers from the chief priests and Pharisees, cometh thither with lanterns and torches and weapons. 4 Jesus therefore, <u>knowing all things that should come upon him</u>, went forth, and said unto them, Whom seek ye? 5 They answered him, Jesus of Nazareth. Jesus saith unto them, <u>I am he</u>. And Judas also, which betrayed him, stood with them. 6 <u>As soon then as he had said unto them, I am he</u>,"they" <u>went backward</u>, and <u>fell to the ground</u>. 7 Then <u>asked he them again</u>, Whom seek ye? And they said, Jesus of Nazareth. 8 Jesus answered, <u>I have told you</u> that <u>I am he</u>: if therefore ye seek me, let these go their way: 9 That the saying might be fulfilled, which he spake, <u>Of them which thou gavest</u> me have <u>I lost none</u>. For in that day was the prophecy fulfilled which He spoke of in Luke 20: 17 And he beheld them, and said, What is this then that is written, The <u>stone</u> which the <u>builders</u> <u>rejected</u>, the same is become the <u>head</u> of the <u>corner</u>?

To this cause is it written that when the Lord said; I am He, <u>they</u> went <u>backward</u> and <u>fell</u> to the <u>ground</u>. This showing that a <u>hidden</u> <u>event</u> took place at that <u>time</u>, even unto the <u>High</u> <u>Ones</u> and the <u>builders</u> that <u>believed</u> Him <u>not</u>, that He was the Son of God foretold to come. For you see the builders and the High Ones and the beast with seven Heads are one. Nevertheless, the Kingdom in the Lord's generation was the sixth Kingdom and the time of the deadly wound which did come. Now in Rev.: 13: 11 it speaks of another Beast that comes, which would become the seventh Kingdom:

11 And I beheld another beast coming up out of the earth; and he had two horns like a lamb, and he spake as a dragon. 12 And he exerciseth all the power of the <u>first beast before him</u>, and causeth the earth and them which dwell therein to worship the <u>first beast</u>, whose <u>deadly wound</u> was <u>healed</u>.

This again being the seventh Kingdom upon the earth. And the seventh kingdom is our time and our generation, even the one that must <u>continue</u> for a <u>short space</u>. And the <u>eighth</u>, which is of the seven is the <u>Kingdom</u> spoken of in the <u>lasts days</u>, which comes <u>after</u> the <u>great calamity</u>, when the time of the two witnesses to finish their testimony before the God of the earth, even a Great City like no other. Rev. 11:7

11: 7 And when they shall have finished their testimony, the beast that ascendeth out of the bottomless pit shall make war against them, and shall overcome them, and kill *them. 8 And their dead bodies shall lie in the street of the <u>Great City</u>, which spiritually is called Sodom and Egypt, where also our Lord was crucified.*

For you see the High Ones are the builders of this City and it will be seen as the great Kingdom that has no end. That it should stand through the millennium and be brought into eternity by the Lord. For they shall show themselves as the fulfilling of the millennium of peace and the true knowledge of God's word. But it is not so. For the Great Red Dragon is its Authority, Power, and Seat. And God's Wrath shall fall on it. As it was written in Daniel: 2:43

2:43 And whereas thou sawest <u>iron mixed with miry clay</u>, they shall <u>mingle themselves</u> with the <u>seed of men</u>: but they shall <u>not cleave one</u> to <u>another</u>, even as iron is not mixed with clay. 44 And in the days of these kings <u>shall</u> the <u>God</u> of <u>heaven set up a kingdom</u>, which shall <u>never</u> be <u>destroyed</u>: and the <u>kingdom shall not be left to other people</u>, but it shall break in pieces and consume all these <u>kingdoms</u>, and it shall stand for ever.

This meaning that this kingdom (that is to say this people) shall not remain here on this earth, but rather removed from this world (Kingdom) unto the world to come, which has no end. And to this cause it says the Kingdom shall not be left to other people. And that it is not a people that shall break in pieces these Kingdoms, but rather the Kingdom of God shall destroy them. Even the Great White Throne Judgment. For the dream also showed this: and the <u>stone</u> that <u>smote</u> the <u>image</u> became a <u>great mountain</u>, and <u>filled</u> the <u>whole earth</u>. This being the time of the Second Resurrection and the <u>harvest</u> of the <u>sixty fold</u> and the <u>thirty fold</u> upon the <u>whole earth</u>. Yea, even the <u>stranger</u> who shall be <u>added</u> to the <u>fold</u>. Because it is the will of our Heavenly Father that not one of these little ones should perish. And the <u>vision</u> is <u>certain</u>, and the <u>interpretation sure</u>.

Amen.......

~ *Spirit* ~

Matt. 6:25 *Therefore I tell you, do not worry about your life, what you will eat or what you will drink, or about your body, what you will wear. Is not life more than food, and the body more than clothing?*

Just as the body can live without clothing, life can be without this body, but not in this kingdom. But know this, your life or should I say your conscience lives beyond this kingdom. Consider what the Lord said in John: 3:8

> *3:8 The wind bloweth where it listeth, and thou hearest the sound thereof, but canst not tell whence it cometh, and whither it goeth: so is every one that is born of the Spirit.*

What that is saying is that you don't remember where you are from or where you are going, but that you did come from some other place to this one and then you shall be yet going again, but where and to whom? I say these things to make you consider the things you do and say and how this will govern your state of being here and now. And where you will be going in the world to come. Let me explain. Life is not the body nor the things the body needs for itself. The body is the medium or that which the life passes through. The manifestation of life. And the very life is Spirit. Now your mind, not your brain, which houses your mind, is made up of thought energy. Which in itself is not body (has no mass), but certainly exist and we ourselves make it self evident that it is so. As it is said: I think, therefore I am. Nevertheless, this thought which we are is indeed spirit, but not true Spirit. The life of Christ Jesus was and is true Spirit, because he knew where he was from and where he was going. As it is written in John: 8:55

> *8:55 Yet ye have not known him; but I know him: and if I should say, I know him not, I shall be a liar like unto you: but I know him, and keep his saying.*

Now when He appears unto us, then we will become like Him.. Then shall we become True Spirit. But until then we must follow Him and His sayings or else we will part from Him and be governed by another, which is from below. For we will do according by whom we are governed. As I said before, thought is spirit and we can not tell if a thought is of our spirit or another's. Now if we say to ourselves, this was my thought. Then it becomes ours and therefore a part of our spirit and we are bound by it. That is to say, we will fulfill it or do it. This is why the Lord said in Matt.: 5:28

5:28 But I say unto you that whosoever looketh on a woman to lust after her hath committed adultery with her already in his heart.

Know then that what I'm saying to you is truth and <u>guard</u> your spirit and <u>rebuke</u> that which you know is not of our Lord or His ways. This is why we must eat the Lord's flesh and drink His blood or else we will have no part of Him in us. And how then and what then will we compare our thoughts to? And how will we know what manner of spirit we are adding to ourselves and thereby the judgment also. Another example the Lord gave us is written in Matt.: 17:12

17:12 But I say unto you, <u>That Elias is come already, and they knew him not</u>, but have done unto him whatsoever they listed. Likewise shall also the Son of man suffer of them.

This showing that John the Baptist and Elias were of the same spirit and knew it not, because John was asked and he answered with a no. Yet the Lord said it was so. For you see spirit and thought are the same substance. Consider what the Lord said about the words which He spoke. He said they were spirit. John: 6:63

6:63 It is the spirit that quickeneth; the flesh profiteth nothing: <u>the words that I speak unto you, they are spirit, and they are life</u>.

The words that one speaks are thoughts that are then spoken. The question is who's ? Should you speak them, then they are yours. Should you believe them, then they are yours. If you rebuke them, then they are some one else's. It is by this means that a deceiving spirit enters into a man without him knowing and talks with him as if it was the man's thought. Even as it was with Peter when he spoke to Jesus in Mark: 8:33

8:33 But when he had turned about and looked on his disciples, <u>he rebuked Peter, saying, Get thee behind me, Satan</u>: for thou savourest not the things that be of God, but the things that be of men..

Peter heard the words within himself and believed it was his thoughts, but Jesus said it was Satan's words which Peter spoke and <u>rebuked them from him</u>. For Peter knew not that it was not of his spirit and was willing through deception to act upon them believing that he was doing good. And again in Luke: 9:54

9:54 And when his disciples James and John saw this, they said, Lord, wilt thou that we command fire to come down from heaven, and consume them, even as Elias did? Luke 9:55

9:55 But he turned, and <u>rebuked them</u>, and said, <u>Ye know not what manner of spirit ye are of</u>.

To this end do I say, take heed to the thoughts that you hear and examine them as to whether they are pertaining to the Spirit of God or the things of men. If they are of man, then be wise as a serpent and gentle as a dove and no harm shall come of it. And if it be of God, then search the scripture and with fasting and prayer you shall know of whom the doctrine is of. For God reveals unto His children His Truth. For he who ask in faith and love shall receive patience. Seek with patience and you shall find truth. Knock and you shall stand within the Holy Place and wisdom and understanding shall be yours. For God has set a time for everything under the sun. Even a time when you can find the things concerning Him and a time when you can not. As it is written in Luke: 10:24

> *10:24 For I tell you, that <u>many prophets</u> and <u>kings</u> have desired to <u>see those things</u> which <u>ye see</u>, and have <u>not seen them</u>; and to <u>hear those things</u> which <u>ye hear</u>, and have <u>not heard them</u>.*

So be of good cheer for the time is now to seek the truth of what things should come shortly, which is the Lord and His Glory and be not dismayed by the things that do appear. For outwardly there will be much sorrow and many lives will be taken from our sight, yet I tell you many lives shall pass from death unto life in this day and to those who remain do I say, hold fast to this Gospel and seek the Lord while He can be found and be added to the Kingdom of Life while there is still time. For the time of the two (2) Witnesses Is the last of the time to be saved and the time of the Rapture is the beginning of their Testimony, which is even now at the door. Therefore take notice of the time and season and enter-in to life and depart from the way of death, which is unbelief of the Lord's Gospel. For I tell you a Truth, it will be easier now to believe the Gospel then it will after the coming of this <u>Man</u> of <u>Sin</u> and his revealing of himself, which is to say coming in <u>His</u> own <u>Name</u>. Behold, it is His <u>Time</u> and He <u>Must Come!!</u> Therefore, remember from hence you have fallen and repent and believe this Gospel. Do you not yet understand ? This <u>Good News</u> has come for you so that you might receive it and be made 'alive' and added to the Kingdom of <u>Life</u>. In this <u>Truth</u> you can possess your own soul. As it is written in Luke: 21:19

> *21:19 In your patience possess ye your souls. For what shall a man exchange for his soul? And what will a man have if he should gain the whole world, but lose his own soul?*

Brethren, I desire you not to be ignorant in this matter. We are three fold in our making. Even as God is three fold in His nature. We are body, spirit and soul. Our body can not live without our spirit. For the body is an image of the spirit and draws life from it. And our spirit draws its power from our soul. The soul is that number or name which God has given you from the beginning when He made all things. Jer. 1:5

1:5 *Before I formed thee* in the belly *I knew thee*; and *before thou camest forth out of the womb* I sanctified thee, and I ordained thee a prophet unto the nations. It is by this truth that He says unto every man: I remember you. For He is a God of order. As the Lord said in Matt.: 13:18

18 *But there shall not an hair of your head perish.*

Therefore every hair on your head is numbered. Nevertheless, this soul can be Dead or Alive. If it belongs to the God of the earth. Then it is Dead. If it belongs to the God of heaven and earth. Then it is Alive. He knows us by our Name. This Soul (Name) is as the Angels of God, but truly they are His Children. The Little Ones of God. For truly they are Lead by a Child. For <u>He</u> is known as such by <u>His Father</u>. Isa. 11:6

11:6 *The wolf also shall dwell with the lamb, and the leopard shall lie down with the kid; and the calf and the young lion and the fatling together;* <u>*and a little child shall lead them*</u>.

As I was saying, the soul will determine what your spirit will draw from for its strength and wisdom. If our soul is in heaven before the Father then we will receive of Him. As it is written in John: 3:13

3:13 *And no man hath ascended up to heaven, but he that came down from heaven, even the* <u>*Son of man which is in heaven*</u>.

This saying that Son of man was on the earth and His soul was in heaven before the Father. And again in Matt.: 18:10

18:10 *Take heed that ye despise not one of these* <u>*little ones*</u>; for I say unto you, <u>*That in heaven their angels do always behold the face of my Father which is in heaven.*</u>

Now some would say: its says their angel not their soul is in heaven and it means their guardian angel. But the literal translation would be <u>living soul</u>. For to God the Angels are His messengers and not His children. And His children are <u>as</u> the Angels of God, but not them. They are different and they should be. For each have their purpose. Therefore know the meaning of this saying and understand what the soul is and then you'll also know where it is. If our soul is of the Earth and before the God of this world. Then we will receive of Him. To this cause we <u>Must</u> be born again from above, which is within and then we become 'alive' and yet <u>Death</u> will follow you around as long as you are here. Therefore you must continue to walk in <u>Faith</u> to stay 'awake'. Once you become alive, you can not die, but you can sleep. It is the will of the Father that not one of these <u>little ones</u> should perish. He will never leave you if you have truly given Him your Heart. But you can be <u>Dead in Christ</u>! Either <u>bodily</u> or <u>spiritually</u>. Bodily being, of course when your spirit has parted from the flesh. Either because of judgment (failure to be fruitful in that life) or reward (bringing forth fruitfulness). For we live to be fruitful and this is our purpose in being upon the earth during the Resurrection. It was so in the First Resurrection (Righteousness). And likewise in the Second Resurrection (Damnation). For they which lived not for a thousand years are raised up unto Damnation. For it is their just reward. Yet there is a Great multitude who come forth from the Great Tribulations which also receive their fruitfulness. Did not the Lord say: He who is forgiven much shall love much. He who has an ear to hear let him hear what the Spirit saith. Now to understand being Dead in Christ spiritually let us Consider 1Cor.5:5

5:5 To deliver such an one unto <u>Satan</u> for the <u>destruction</u> of the <u>flesh</u>, that the <u>spirit</u> may be <u>saved</u> in the day of the Lord Jesus. For if this one is a believer of Christ and has fallen into deception of other doctrines or has become blinded by his senses or has become offended in Christ. For all these things are governed by one's spirit and then seen outwardly . Then he is in danger of losing his fruitfulness thereby falling into judgment, which is for the Lord and His judgment seat to give counsel and reward and as such the following will apply to him. As it is written in Matt. 18:14

> *18:14 Even so it is not the will of your Father which is in heaven, that one of these little ones should perish. 15 Moreover if thy brother shall trespass against thee, go and tell him his fault between <u>thee</u> and <u>him alone</u>: if he shall hear thee, thou hast <u>gained</u> thy <u>brother</u>. 16 But if he will not hear thee, then take with thee one or two more, that in the mouth of two or three witnesses every word may be established. 17 And if he shall neglect to hear them, tell it unto the church: but if he neglect to hear the church, let him be unto thee as a <u>heathen man and a publican</u>. 18 Verily I say unto you, Whatsoever ye shall bind on earth shall be bound in heaven and whatsoever ye shall loose on earth shall be loosed in heaven. 19 Again I say unto you, That if two of you shall agree on earth as touching any thing that they shall ask, it shall be done for them of my Father which is in heaven. 20 For where two or three are gathered together in my name, there am I in the midst of them.*

So then if he is to be to you as a <u>heathen man</u>, then it is the Lord and His doing that shall keep him and he has become <u>Dead</u> in <u>Christ</u>. And you need to remember that you can not always know what manner of spirit you are presently of and to this cause become deceived and react to another spirit and not your true self that the Lord has made of you when He made you a new creature. This is how we go in and out of pastures. And why we need a mediator between God and us. And the reason that the Lord is made strong in our weakness.

For all these things must be accomplished in this Kingdom and in this body before we can become the Children of God. For we must become like Him, the Lord Christ Jesus. Both in body and in spirit. Bodily, because His body became Glorified and when we see Him we shall be changed and made like Him . And spiritually, because He will write His New Name upon us and we will Know Him. And in knowing Him we will know where we are from and where we shall always be.This making us True Spirit as He is. To this cause we shall drink of the waters of Life Freely. Knowing our Father, the Lord and His God, The Holy Spirit, even the Spirit of Truth, {God Almighty}. Until then let us be mindful of the Lord's ways and keep our spirit subjected to Him. That we might know His chastising and give Him our reverence. For in doing so we become witnesses unto God and His Christ and He gives us His Power to become Sons Of God as He Is. Even so Oh Lord.

Amen and Amen.......

~ Honor ~

John 5:44 *How can ye believe, which receive <u>honour</u> one of another, and seek not the <u>honour</u> that cometh from <u>God only</u>?*

What manner of <u>honor</u> is it that comes from <u>God only</u> ? First we must consider what <u>honor</u> is before we can begin to find the <u>honor</u> that comes from <u>God only</u>. We say honor is respect one from the other also dignity, praise and in some cases even worship. And it is so, even to the latter, but men do often make the appearance of honor outwardly and inwardly the intent has no honor in it at all. Therefore, let us state what manner of honor we speak of here. The honor that men are willing to die for and dedicate their lives to, even though it is from one man to another. For the honor that a man can display toward God is greater then what he is able to show to another man. Because God will magnify the honor a man may give to Him. And the last state of the man is greater then the first, because God has added His Honor unto it. So you see, honor from God comes only when we <u>ask</u> and <u>want</u> God to use us openly for His will. And in doing so you will serve His children not looking for <u>praise</u> or <u>return</u>. For if God works in you openly He has already honored you by reason of His presents. Because the source of all things has been seen in you. To this cause did the Lord say if any man have <u>need</u> of such things as you have <u>and he ask</u> of you then <u>refuse him not</u>. Do not be confused between <u>need</u> and <u>want</u>. Because there are many who want, but need it not. Do you wish to serve <u>God</u> or <u>man</u> ? If you <u>serve man</u> then you serve his <u>master</u>! And in like manner, if you serve God then you serve His Children. For God gives His kingdom unto His Children. Did not the Lord give us an example? Give to those that can not return thanks unto you and your heavenly Father will give you that which you need as well as the desires of your heart. This is how you can serve God and not man. If you should give in the name of a prophet or righteous man, even a disciple and then in the passing of time you find yourself in need of something or someone's help, your heavenly Father will give to you accordingly. For a man's works do follow him. As it is written in Matt.: 10:41

> *10:41 He that receiveth a prophet in the name of a prophet shall receive a prophet's reward, and he that receiveth a righteous man in the name of a righteous man shall receive a righteous man's reward. And whosoever shall give to drink unto one of these little ones a cup of cold water only in the name of a disciple, verly I say unto you, he shall in no wise lose his reward.*

For if you truly honor God by reason of your service to Him then He will honor you the more. But how do you truly honor God in your service to Him ? For there is One who will judge your service to Him. And this is the manner this One judges. First he will give you opportunity to gain praise from others, within or without God's Name. See that you do it not, but humble yourself and say, we are unprofitable servants: we have done that which was our duty to do. If you are able to believe this and there by able to live it and walk in it then God has honored you already. Then this one will remind you of things you have done for friends for friendship sake or even family or loved ones. And afterwards cause you to believe you have need or perhaps want of something that your friend or loved ones have or even received of you. And when you ask of it from your friend or loved ones they will at first say no I can not. Let not this offend you or cause you to ask again for that which is yours. For if you truly have need of that which is yours, will not God return it to you in the same manner in which you gave it ? Yes, Indeed He will. And if you thought you had need of it, but you were led to believe so and you don't become offended, then the honor that comes from God only will comfort you and your friend or loved ones will come to you offering their honor to you and asking for your forgiveness. And again God is honoring you in them also. This is the honor that comes from God only. And as I had said, to truly give Honor unto God is by letting His Love come through you unto others. This is done by willingly allowing God's Love to move in your heart and then you acting upon it toward another. For God searches for such and they do Honor Him. If you should find yourself walking down the street one day and you come upon a small young lad who has tripped and hurt himself and you feel sorrow and concerned about him. This is the spirit of God moving within you, because He Loves His Children. And if you should help this lad and not look for thanks or praise then you have the opportunity to give God honor by realizing that what you have just felt and reacted to was the spirit of God in you and give Him the praise and thanks and glory and He will openly Honor you. For God truly receives His pleasure from such and they likewise will find this joy. This is not the joy that comes from the world, which will fade away quickly, but a joy that will stay with you and keep you, even in great distress and sorrows. For what does a man believe, but that which he lives and what does he possess, but the things he gathers unto himself. Therefore take hold of this concept and live it and you shall be gathering unto yourself heavenly things that shall remain with you no matter where you might go. And you shall be comforted no matter what Evil might seek to harm you or take from you. As it is written in Mat.: 6:19

> *6:19 Lay not up for yourselves treasures upon the earth, where moth and rust doth corrupt and where thieves break through and steal. But lay up for yourselves treasures in heaven, where neither moth nor rust doth corrupt, and where thieves do not break through nor steal.*

For that which God gives you is yours and no one can take it from you. And if you wish to give it to another, then give it in the same manner that it was given unto you and it shall remain yours, because God shall return it unto you in its time. Do not believe this in the appearance of things, because the Kingdom of God comes not by observation but in

<u>Faith</u> and it is so and can be seen as such. Now as to this One who judges, he will also make opportunity to persuade you into believing that if you do something for someone else so that they will do something for you and that this is an honorable thing before God and God's Honor will be added unto it. It is not so ! And if a man should give his services in exchange for that which was done for him only because he feels indebted to him. Is it not the same ? But if a man should do good works for another because of the need of things and he who receives then gives thanks to him. Now the honor mentioned here is the honor from one man to another and it is good and acceptable unto just men and God is not against it. So give what is man's unto man and what is God's unto God. If you can not see the difference between God's Honor and man's honor then how will you find the patience to receive God's Honor. For His Honor comes in fullness of time and the test of time can not change it, but unbelief will delay it. Remember, there is One who desires to replace this <u>honor</u> with <u>offense</u>, which brings forth hurt, anger, revenge, hatred and disbelief. If you believe this One who judges you then this judgment is then measured again unto you. Who then shall give you what is yours? And how then can you receive this <u>honor</u> that comes from <u>God Only</u> ? You must seek His Honor if you wish to receive it. There is also a difference between His Honor and His Grace and you should not confuse the two or else the Evil One will use it against you. As you know, Grace is unmerited and comes without <u>favor</u>. And this <u>Honor</u> of <u>God's</u> can <u>not come without favor</u>. For It is God magnifying what you have given Him unto you. This work of His can not be called Grace, because His Grace need not be magnified. For He said: My Grace is sufficient. Therefore the honor that you have given Him by reason of your love for Him is indeed magnified and measured again unto you. This Honor can Only come from God. I give you a mystery, Faith through love will bring <u>patience</u>, which will bring <u>understanding</u> and from this <u>you</u> can <u>give</u> Him Honor. This is not a thing of or a part of Salvation, but of Glory. And God is worthy of it and makes his Children able to receive it from Him worthily. And in receiving it so also do they find His Joy, which will keep them in their time of trouble. Even in the time of Great Blasphemies. When this One who comes in all Lying Wonders causes as many as will hear him to fall into his captivity and not see the time and season they are in. To this cause say I unto you, make not judgments of others, least they are your children, because God has given you the commandment to teach your children, which requires you to judge them. And He sees teaching as an honorable work and will bless you in the doing because in His coming He also came to teach. As to others, witness their works, but judge them not and pray always for patience which keeps you and strengthens you by reason of sight because as you see the end of such works, it will always show what manner of deeds it is of and thereby removing the need for judgment and also teaching you concerning the good ways of life which will increase your wisdom and the Lord's peace in you. Because He teaches us through these works which come that we might become more like Him. For with this understanding we are then made able to give Him Honor. And by doing so He will measure again this Honor unto us and as I said before the last state of the man is greater then the first. Therefore if you truly seek God's Honor and come to know this Glory and this Honor that comes from <u>God Only</u>, you shall

then find the strength and the ability to comfort many in their times of need, because God has given you His comforting, because of your Love for Him. He to whom it is given, let him receive it. For he will give, even as it was given unto him. And God shall be glorified in him, even as God shall glorify him in it. For this is the Honor that comes from God Only. If you find it not in this kingdom, be of good cheer for you shall obtain it in the world to come. Because we will be like Him in the world to come. For God has promised to give us the true riches in the Everlasting Kingdom and He has made a way, yes a sure way. From everlasting to everlasting is the Lord our God and we are in Him. Let us be glad and rejoice for our redemption has drawn near before us. Even so Oh Lord, thy Grace is sufficient unto us.

Amen and Amen.......

Children of the
~ Resurrection ~

Children of the resurrection of the latter days. Have remembrance of the works that the Lord has performed for you. For He prepared this place and this nation for you so that you might have life and have it more abundantly. For this nation is the Camp of the Saints. For she has within her gates the human rights of justice, freedom, the pursuit of happiness and love for equality of all mankind. For it is in her that the promise of the fruitfulness of the gentiles has been given. And also the prophecy which the Lord gave concerning any nation that would come against her would be broken. And history has shown this to be true. Consider Japan, Germany and the cold war of Russia. For the prophecy was directed in part toward those who would come against her. Let not misunderstanding come from this statement. For God is Faithful in His Word, but we are not. For we have had our share of blunders. But there is yet a part of this prophecy to be fulfilled and it shall come to pass. As it is written in Matt.:

> 21:44 And whosoever shall fall on this stone shall be broken: but on whomsoever it shall fall, it will grind him to powder.

For I tell you a truth it is within this generation that this shall be fulfilled in your sight and shortly after this shall the Calamity and then the One World Order (government) should come to pass before you. Nevertheless, God has blessed this nation and has kept her, because His laws and precepts have been found in her. And the Great Commission has been fulfilled in her. That is to say, God's Word and His Works have been accomplished through her children, which have gone out unto the uttermost part of the earth in His Name. Even as He commanded His disciples. And this thing we call Christianity was brought here to be nourished that she should once again stand before the face of the Serpent.

> (Rev. 12:1 And there appeared a great wonder in heaven; a woman clothed with the sun, and the moon under her feet, and upon her head a crown of twelve stars: And Rev.12:14; 14 And to the woman were given two wings of a great eagle, that she might fly into the wilderness, into her place, where she is nourished for a time, and times, and half a time, from the face of the serpent.)

For her works have been found in this nation and this is our Greatness. Yet I remind you these works are found in you and not made by you. Therefore, honor God for this by keeping His Name and precepts in your laws and in your doings or else He will part from you and shorten your days as a nation and will send an Angel who will cry out and say: come out of her my people. Children of the resurrection let not this happen without a fight. For it is in the works of trying to save her that the Lord shall bring you, His people, out of her before the falling, they who shall enter into the Rapture. And to those who remain and witness the Great Tribulation, they shall see a new City rise up in its Greatness, but Great shall be the fall of it and short shall be the days of it. For the God of the earth shall be the Father of it. And it is here that the nations shall become angry when they see the Lord's wrath coming upon it. Now the fight I speak of is the voting power of the people to keep upright men in our places of government and order. And that we should pray continually for those that work for our behalf. For I tell you a truth, the Angel spoken of in Rev. 18:1 is come and is coming. What then shall we do? We should remember our beginning as a nation. Because our founding forefathers were given our documents of government from our Heavenly Father. (Declaration of Independence, The Constitution and The Bill of Rights). And to this cause have we included "In God We Trust". For our forefathers knew it would not work without Him. And they were right. For time has bore witness of it. Because these documents given us from above have survived all the trials that have been put against it. But now is the time of Great Blasphemies. Rev. 13:6 . And the documents we hold precious are being divided and made corruptible. And we are turning away from its precepts. For the Spirit of subtleness has crept into our lives so that each one of us, without knowing it is seeking the interest of the self only and causing all of us to go our separate ways. No longer looking at the whole, but only the part. Have we not been divided ? And a house divided must fall. Consider Rev.: 17:18

18 And the woman which thou sawest is that great city, which reigneth over the kings of the earth.

If you can receive it, this woman, which is also the whore is the camp of the saints in its state of falling. And In Rev. 17:12

12 And the ten horns which thou sawest are ten kings, which have received no kingdom as yet; but receive power as kings one hour with the beast. 13 These have one mind, and shall give their power and strength unto the beast. 14 These shall make war with the Lamb, and the Lamb shall overcome them: for he is Lord of Lords, and King of Kings: and they that are with him are called, and chosen, and faithful. And in Rev. 17:16

16 And the ten horns which thou sawest upon the beast, these shall hate the whore, and shall make her desolate and naked, and shall eat her flesh, and burn her with fire. And in Rev. 17:15

15 And he saith unto me, The waters which thou sawest where the whore sitteth, are peoples, and multitudes, and nations, and tongues.

So you see, if the <u>kings</u> desire to make the <u>woman desolate</u> and <u>burn her with fire</u>, then <u>she</u> is not one of them, but rather <u>she</u> has been <u>taken by the beast</u> and is being <u>carried off to the slaying</u>. Don't you see?

This nation or woman has been deceived and has become bedfellows unto the wicked. But the ten (10) kings are also doing as God has made them to do for <u>His Will</u> . Rev.: 17:17

17 For God hath put in their hearts to fulfill <u>his will</u>, and to <u>agree</u>, and <u>give</u> their kingdom unto the <u>beast</u>, until the words of God shall be fulfilled.

And you shall shortly understand why God should do such a thing. For you see, all these things are the beginnings of sorrows that have come upon her (the woman). As concerning our nation and our present time I say again, <u>she must fall</u>. Not from the doing of another nation, but as an act of God. Do you not yet see ? We have been putting men in Moses Seat (law makers) who have no regard of God in them. To this cause has the Name of God been removed and is being removed from our places of honor (Courts and Government bodies). And our places of teaching (schools and colleges). And soon, if not stopped, radio and television, even our churches. For these kings can influence those setting in our seats of government, but we should the more influence them, because of the power of the peoples vote. Consider this: When it speaks of the 10 kings, then it speaks of the middle east. Isn't this the land of which our Lord walked ? And it is the land where God's words are fulfilled. For all these things <u>must</u> come to pass to fulfill the words of God. Even as it was <u>needful</u> for this <u>nation</u> (the woman) to go and make <u>war</u> with <u>one who desired</u> to <u>eat</u> the <u>woman's flesh</u> and to <u>burn her with fire</u> and to make <u>her desolate</u>. Our being there is <u>required of us</u>. For in being there we served (2) two purposes. To <u>fulfill God's words</u> and to <u>bear</u> the <u>lesser of (2) two evils</u>. For had we not moved against the works being done there, then the <u>greater</u> would the <u>burning with fire</u> have been to <u>her</u> and the <u>greater</u> the <u>nakedness</u>. But as I have said, it is not these things that shall make her fall and not rise again. It is God's wrath unto those who have corrupted this <u>Great City</u>, even a <u>nation</u>. For the <u>Camp</u> of the <u>Saints</u> and this <u>Great City</u> are indeed one. And the beginning of sorrows are upon <u>her</u>. But the <u>Greater</u> comes in the <u>Calamity</u>. Therefore, say I unto you: Come out of her my people. But if you want to keep what you have until the <u>time appointed</u>. Then <u>Honor God</u> and <u>His Name</u> among you and let not these <u>men</u> with the <u>mark</u> of the <u>beast</u> take it from you before the time of its receiving unto God. For the Glory of the nations are received unto heaven in its time. Nevertheless, if you will not hear and therefore not do as you should. It shall be taken from you. And then who shall give you what is yours ? For the workmen is worthy of his hire. And his works do follow him. Once again I say: <u>Children</u> of the <u>Camp</u> of the <u>Saints</u>, hear the calling of the <u>Spirit</u> of <u>Truth</u> and lift up again the <u>Name</u> of <u>God</u> in your <u>laws</u> and in your <u>doings</u> or else <u>He will</u> <u>part from you</u> and <u>not</u> <u>Rebuke the Destroyer</u>. Even so Oh Lord <u>awaken them</u> that they should have <u>remembrance of thee</u>. And that thy <u>Grace</u> should abound in them as they call unto thee in this day which is before us.

Amen.......

Citizens of the City of Lights. Do you not know how your nation's system works? You the people elect those who serve you. And if they serve you then you must tell them what is required. I tell you to eat the flesh of your nation, that is to say learn of her ways and use them or else another shall do it for you. When I say her I speak of the laws and the law makers of this Great Country. God gave us this land and this system of standards that we might govern ourselves and give Him the Glory. And if we give Him the Glory then our churches would grow and the people would not lose sight of Him and His Name would be honored among us always. But if we become divided and remove His Name and His Works from among us. And make it a law not to speak His Name unto His people. Then we shall become those whom the Lord spoke of in Matt.: 7:6

7:6 Cast not your pearls before swine. Least they trample them under their feet and turn again and rend you.

For we need not lose that which we have if we will remember what our founding fore-fathers knew and put in the body of their work, which was and is and should always be: "In God We Trust". It has been said that approximately eighty five per cent (85%) of the popula-tion of this country are Christians. How then is it possible that God's Name is being ques-tioned when it is by His Name this nation came into being and was being relied upon for its foundation ? Because we have let other men take our places of honor to themselves and made it a den of thieves. For they do sell themselves to obtain their places or they will be forced to cover their own shame because they have not the love of God in their works. And yet must persuade many that they are able to accomplish much by reason of their works. And I tell you a truth, look at their works, for our laws are making things that are wrong as though they are right. For example; Abortion is used to cover up and hide many wrong doings, of which it would take much writing to speak of all of it. And in truth, such a thing should be used only to save a woman's life because of complications, which would cause her death. If a woman for what ever the reason did not want her children. She should not have them killed. Are not there many who desire children and can not have them ? And are not there many being killed be-cause some hide their shame and consider not life as a precious thing given of God ? Yet they do consider their lives worthy enough to keep or perhaps they perceive like some that life does not start until after the birth canal. How is it that they do not understand that life here begins at the time of conception? I tell you a truth, they stay in darkness so that their deeds do not appear to them for what they are. That is to say, evil. Again I say, we are responsible for our laws because we either elected those who are in Moses seat or we do nothing to remove one who uses the office of service wrongly. We as a people should hold accountable those whom we put in office. And if we do, then we will require service of them in our behalf instead of them making our law to suite themselves and denying us the right to worship our God who gave us, all of us, this nation and the fruitfulness thereof. Hear me Oh Citizens of the Camp of the Saints. If you are the Children of God and if you are His Churches. Then rise up and do more then say, I am a Christian, but rather say, because I am a Christian I will do my duty and <u>sleep not</u> but <u>watch</u> and I will see what <u>manner</u> of <u>spirit</u> is trying to govern our God given country and give him not room to corrupt our laws or to make us forget <u>who</u> to <u>Honor</u> for the rights and the freedom which we take for granted each day of our lives in this Great Country of ours.

Amen and Amen.......

Remember this, our founding forefathers said: <u>In God We Trust</u>. As I said before, the very foundation of our country rest on the precepts and morality of the teachings of God. And through men who believe by reason of it. Remove this from our system of Government and we shall fall before our time of being received unto heaven. And there shall be weeping and gnashing of teeth as they are being cast into utter darkness. Because they would not hear nor would they believe that it was needful to restore the Name of God in their laws and in their doings. And they made laws to glory in their shame and to be ashamed of God's Glory and removed His Name from among themselves. Let them <u>not</u> do to you what they want to do to themselves. For if you let them, <u>they will do it</u> and rejoice in the doing. And if it is done, there will be "<u>no undoing</u>". Therefore the Spirit saith unto the churches: Principal of the flock, speak unto your congregation as you have been doing in part, but unify the churches in this matter and be one voice onto the people and the Lord shall straight way accomplish it. For we are His people and <u>He will rebuke this spirit</u> and <u>restore His Spirit among us</u>. Even the Spirit of Truth. For this nation is made up of many kindred and peoples and tongues, even as it is written in Revelation. Yes with believers and non believers. For God has brought us together to do His Works among us. For woe unto the world for offense, but the world needs offenses. For it is in such things that God fulfills His Words. Even so learn from a parable the Lord gave us. Where unto shall I liken the Kingdom of God ? It is like leaven, which a woman took and hid in three measures of meal, till the whole was leaven. Here is where the saying is true <u>again</u>. The woman is the church and the three measures of meal are the <u>peoples</u> of this nation (<u>kindreds</u> and <u>tongues</u>) and the leaven is the word of God and His Works being made manifest. Nevertheless, we must not let the non believer change our laws and prevent us from worshipping our God openly. They should not change our way, but we should teach them the way that is right by using the unity of the people who are believers. For God will work in us His Will. Even so oh Lord it is Your Works that accomplishes all things and <u>our praise</u> unto <u>you</u> that is <u>Your Pleasure</u>. Let me explain something, there is a difference between men with the mark of the beast and men deceived by the mark of the beast. Men with the mark of the beast have no regard or concern of God in their heart or their deeds. Whereas a man deceived by the mark of the beast will close his heart so as to agree by reason of deception, but his heart will remain true because he is only dead in Christ. For you see, if you have given Him your heart, then He will keep it for you and will not let it fail you or let it become corrupt. Is He not your Lord ? Did He not say, Lo I am with you always, even to the end of the world? Therefore, unto this one and in his time of calling, his mouth shall speak the fullness of his heart and he will not receive the mark of the beast . Not on his hand, that is to say the works of his hand. Nor on his forehead, that is to say in his thoughts and desires that he would wish to fulfill it. For they that receive it are destine to it because He the Evil One has already deceived His own and as it is written in Rev. 22:11

11: He that is unjust, let him be unjust still: and he which is filthy, let him be filthy still: and he that is righteous, let him be righteous still: and he that is holy, let him be holy still. Therefore, judge not the man, but consider his fruit and let your witnessing be enough. For the Lord is your strength and will help you concerning these matters. As I said earlier to pray continually for those who work for our behalf. And we should elect those who's fruit lifts up the Name of God both in words and in deeds. For is not the workmen worthy of his hire ? And an upright man loveth his work when he sees the fruit of the Lord in his hands. And he will do much good for the people. Because such a man will have a vision and will seek to fulfill it as he should because it is inspired from above as all good things come from above. Even this testament, which is given to a people that they should know the time and season of which they are presently in. For no man will stir up himself unto God, but God must stir him that he the man might agree and believe and act in Faith. Consider Proverbs: 29:18

18 Where there is no <u>Vision</u>, the people perish: but he that keepeth the law, happy is he.

To this cause saith the Spirit of Truth: Churches of the camp of the saints, even the latter days. Let the <u>Seven Thunders</u> be heard and let them be <u>one voice</u>. For if the <u>people</u> will <u>unite</u> in this cause <u>believing</u> that <u>God</u> will <u>heal</u> them.. Will not His Work in us be yet greater still ? And if He is with us. Who then can be against us ? Let it then be Oh Lord according unto your Grace. And let the <u>Seven Thunders</u> be heard in <u>one voice</u> that we should be <u>one people, under God, indivisible</u>, with <u>liberty</u> and <u>justice</u> for <u>all</u>. Yes, it says all, the just and the unjust, the believer and the unbeliever. Is it not written that God is kind unto the unthankful and to the evil ? Let His Works be done in us as we should be thankful and give Him Praise. For of such are His Children and in <u>Them</u> is <u>His Joy</u>.

Amen and Amen......

~ *Testament Summary* ~

The law and the prophets were until John: since that time the Kingdom of God is preached, and <u>every man</u> presseth into <u>it</u>, Luke 16:16.

This saying that the generation of <u>Christ</u> began the First Resurrection, which was the raising up of <u>all</u> from the time of <u>old</u>, even to the end of <u>His</u> generation. These being the <u>First Fruits</u> and the <u>hundred fold</u> of <u>this harvest time</u>. As Jesus said in Matt. 19:29

> *29 <u>And every one that hath forsaken houses, or brethren, or sisters, or father, or mother, or wife, or children, or lands, for my name's sake, shall receive an hundredfold</u>, and shall inherit everlasting life.*

This showing that the *hundredfold* was applied to His coming. And also in the meaning of the parable of the sower in Matt. 13:23

> *23 But he that received seed into the good ground is he that heareth the word, and understandeth it; which also beareth fruit, and bringeth forth, some an <u>hundredfold</u>, some <u>sixty</u>, some <u>thirty</u>.*

The *hundredfold* speaking of <u>His time</u> and <u>generation</u>. And of course the sixty and thirty fold speaking of the latter days. Nevertheless, The Twelve being the foundation of the Church and as the parable tells it, the servants that bring the guest to the marriage supper. For the First Resurrection was four (4) fold in nature. The first being to build the Church, the second was the receiving of the first fruits, the third to gather all the guest to the marriage supper and the fourth was the millennium of <u>judgment</u> and <u>reward</u>. This came to an end when the fifth trumpet <u>was fulfilled</u>. Nevertheless, when Christ ascended he said he would return to receive them (disciples) to himself so that where He <u>Is</u> <u>there</u> they shall be also. As the Lord said to his disciples: *In my <u>Father's house</u> are <u>many mansions</u>:* For you see it was in one of these places that the marriage supper took place and in another that the twelve thrown <u>judgment</u> and <u>reward</u> was determined. And that the reward was (100) one hundred fold in nature. Now John being the last of the Church foundation to be received ended the <u>Seals</u>, which ended with silence and also the end of the <u>gathering</u> and the formation of the Seven Churches. From that time until the end of the pouring of the Vials was approximately 800 years. For many things were accomplished at this time. Keep in mind what was written in Rev. 16:1

1. And I heard a great voice out of the temple saying to the seven angels, <u>Go "your" ways,</u> and <u>pour</u> out the <u>vials</u> of the wrath of God upon the <u>earth</u>. This time was required to accomplish (2) two things. The first is so that desolation's can be determined. Because of the deeds that Satan and his angels should do because they found themselves upon the earth. And as they would do so should each vial be poured out unto them in Spirit and therefore not seen of men. And the second to close heaven for the preparation of the marriage supper, that is to say those guest who would be called there, yet some would be cast <u>out</u> because of their <u>dishonor</u>. And also that the Church (Bride) should make Herself ready. And then the marriage and the celebration began. Let me also add that there is the <u>church</u> (Heavenly Body) and the remnant (earthly body). Now after all these things then came the millennium, which was <u>judgment</u> and <u>reward</u>. As it is written in John 8:26

> *26 I have many things to <u>say</u> and to <u>judge</u> of you: but <u>he</u> that <u>sent me</u> is <u>true</u>; and I speak to the world those things which I have heard of <u>him</u>.*

And again Rev. 22:12

> *12 And, behold, I come quickly; and my <u>reward</u> is with <u>me</u>, to <u>give every man accord-</u> <u>ing as his work shall be</u>.*

Now the end of the millennium (First Resurrection) and the beginning of the Second Death came approximately in the year of 1914 (Fifth trumpet). At this time there came a movement and an increase of worldly knowledge. The movement was of God pouring <u>His</u> <u>Spirit</u> upon the <u>Churches.</u> And the worldly knowledge, of course came from Satan. From that day to this has been the <u>First Woe</u> ! And the <u>Second Woe</u> begins with the <u>Rapture</u> and the <u>Testimony</u> of the <u>Two Witnesses</u>. Which shall come shortly, for even now it is at the door. You shall see it coming as a <u>Calamity</u>, but you can not stop it or save yourself from it. As it is written in Rev. 16:18

> *18 And there were voices, and thunders, and lightning's; and there was a <u>great earth-</u> <u>quake</u>, such as was not <u>since men were upon the earth</u>, so mighty an earthquake, and so great. 19 And the <u>great city</u> was <u>divided</u> into <u>three parts</u>, and the cities of the na- tions fell: and great Babylon came in remembrance before God, to give unto her the cup of the wine of the fierceness of his wrath. 20 And every island fled away, and the mountains were not found. 21 And there fell upon men a great hail out of heaven, ev- ery stone about the weight of a talent: and men blasphemed God because of the plague of the hail; for the plague thereof was exceeding great.*

For this shall be the beginning of "<u>Their Testimony</u>" that all shall witness so that they might believe the time and season of which they are presently in. Remember then what the Lord said in Luke 21:28

28 And when these things begin to come to pass, then look up, and lift up your heads; for your redemption draweth nigh.

And again in Luke 21:34

34 And take heed to yourselves, lest at any time your <u>hearts</u> be <u>overcharged</u> with <u>sur-feiting</u>, and <u>drunkenness</u>, and <u>cares</u> of <u>this life</u>, and so <u>that day</u> come upon you <u>un-awares</u>. 35 For as a <u>snare</u> shall it <u>come</u> on <u>all</u> them that <u>dwell</u> on the face of the <u>whole earth</u>. 36. Watch ye therefore, and pray always, that ye may be accounted worthy to escape all these things that shall come to pass, and to stand before the Son of man.

For I tell you a truth, even now the signs have begun to appear in the heavens, but they who watch know not what they've been looking at nor will they until this Testament is delivered unto the people to whom it is given. Then shall their hearts fail them because of the things they see coming upon the earth. Even so Oh Lord

Amen and Amen.......

Now the Second Death (Second Resurrection) begins with the (60) sixty fold and then the (30) thirty fold, as the great parable gives it to be. The Rapture is the (60) fold being received and the falling of that Great City the Camp of the Saints, even the fruitfulness of the Gentiles. And the (30) thirty fold come forth from the gathering of the High Ones and the Kings of the earth and the testimony given to them by the (2) Two Witnesses. This of course includes those who go through Great Tribulations, because they would not believe the Gospel as it was given to them. Nor would they take heed to the many signs given to all who were foretold of its coming by reason of this testament and the testimony of the (2) Two Witnesses when they began to speak. For the Churches will reject them when they begin to speak, but the Lord shall draw many unto them before the Calamity is fully come. Now the High Ones and the Kings of the earth in this time shall bring forth a Restoration to the earth, because of the Great Calamity which hurt the earth. And from this comes a Great City unlike any other before this time. For It will be in this Great City (spiritually called Sodom and Egypt) that the (2) Two Witnesses shall <u>stand</u> before the <u>God</u> of the <u>Earth</u> and give their Testimony and display their <u>Authority</u> by reason of the many <u>Plagues</u> which they bring upon the earth. As it is written in Rev. 11:6

6 These have <u>power</u> to <u>shut heaven</u>, that it <u>rain not</u> in the <u>days</u> of their <u>prophecy</u>: and have <u>power</u> over <u>waters</u> to turn them <u>to blood</u>, and to <u>smite</u> the <u>earth</u> with <u>all plagues</u>, as <u>often as they will</u>.

Their time shall begin in the Camp of the Saints and finish in this Great City !!... For when they begin to speak they will make known to those who will hear that the Rapture is at hand and that the God of the earth is coming and is come. And if you will receive it, this testament will be the evidence of the coming of this Angel that is spoken of in Rev. 10:1

> *1. And I saw another mighty angel come down from heaven, clothed with a cloud: and a rainbow was upon his head, and his face was as it were the sun, and his feet as pillars of fire: 2 And he had in his hand a little book open: and he set his right foot upon the sea, and his left foot on the earth, 3 And cried with a loud voice, as when a lion roareth: and when he had cried, seven thunders uttered their voices.* For I tell you a Truth, the voices of the Seven Thunders shall be heard in the time of this testament when it is delivered unto whom it is given, even a people. And also this in Rev. 18:1

> *1 . And after these things I saw another Angel come down from <u>heaven</u>, having great <u>power</u> ; And the <u>earth was lightened</u> with his <u>glory</u>. And he cried mightily with a strong voice, saying, Babylon the great is fallen, is fallen, and is become the <u>habitation</u> of <u>devils</u>, and the hold of every <u>foul Spirit</u>, and a <u>cage</u> of every <u>unclean</u> and <u>hateful bird</u>.* For even now you can see what has happened to this great nation, even the (Camp of the Saints) because of the <u>men</u> with the <u>mark</u> of the <u>beast</u>. For <u>they</u> have <u>changed</u> our <u>laws</u> and <u>removed God</u> from our <u>places</u> of <u>honor</u> (Courts of Justice). And <u>hidden His Name</u> from our <u>children.</u> And we as a people have been letting them do it. Because it is that season and the time is at the door for it to come to pass. Therefore, marvel not at this revealing, but know this, even though it is their time which has come upon us. It can be made shorter, because the Lord has said that he will shorten the days for the Elect sakes. Therefore, hear what the Spirit of Truth saith in this testament and take hold of this truth, because the words and testimony written here in is the crying of this Angel (Spirit) that you might enter-in and be not fearful for the Rapture is before you. Therefore, lift up your eyes unto heaven and rejoice and you shall see the Lord of Glory in the clouds coming and is come. Then after this shall the four Angels be loosened that is written of in Rev. 9:14

> *14. Saying to the sixth angel which had the trumpet, Loose the four angels which are bound in the great river Euphrates. 15 And the four angels were loosed, which were prepared for an hour, and a day, and a month, and a year, for to slay the third part of men.* For it is the coming of this event which will fulfill the prophecy which the Lord made in Matt. 21:44

> *44 And whosoever shall fall on this stone shall be broken: but on whomsoever <u>it shall fall</u>, it will <u>grind him</u> to <u>powder</u>.*

Then shall men's hearts fail them because of that which they see coming upon the earth. For that which they see is the Great Calamity. Nevertheless, these things shall continue for a space of (5) five months then shall the High Ones display their power and strength. After this shall come the Restoration and fulfilling of the (2) Two Witnesses testimony in that Great City where they shall be slain by the <u>God</u> of the <u>Earth</u>. Even so Oh Lord it is by your Power they are given the <u>Spirit</u> of <u>Life.</u> Now as I said concerning the Rapture, which is the (60) sixty fold and then the (30) thirty fold. In Rev. 14:14 it says:

14:14 And I looked and behold a white cloud, and upon the cloud one sat like unto <u>Son</u> of <u>Man</u>, having on his head a golden crown, and in his hand a sharp sickle. And another <u>Angel</u> came out of the <u>temple</u>, crying with a loud voice to him that sat on the cloud, Thrust in thy sickle, and reap: for the <u>time</u> is come for thee to reap; for the harvest of the earth is ripe. And he that sat on the cloud <u>thrust</u> in his sickle on the <u>earth</u>; and the earth was reaped. This being the time of the rapture and the (60) sixty fold to be received by reason of the <u>calamity</u>, which causes a third of man to die. Let this not trouble your heart. For this is not a death unto destruction, but a passing into life everlasting. As the Lord had said: they will pass from Death unto Life. And also Rev. 7:2*

2 And I saw another <u>angel ascending</u> from the <u>east</u>, having the <u>seal</u> of the <u>living God</u>: and he cried with a loud voice to the <u>four angels</u>, to whom it was given <u>to hurt</u> the <u>earth</u> and the <u>sea</u>, 3 Saying, <u>Hurt not</u> the <u>earth</u>, neither the <u>sea</u>, nor the <u>trees, till we have sealed the servants</u> of our <u>God</u> in their foreheads. This <u>hurt</u> spoken of being the time of the <u>calamity</u> (Second Death). And this delay being the time for the marriage of the Lamb (pouring of the vials), as well as the <u>millennium</u> of <u>judgment</u> and <u>reward</u> (First Resurrection), which includes trumpets one (1) thru four(4). Now the event of the Rapture occurs in the Second Death and those who remain on the earth shall behold this One, even a nation. Who shall restore in part the earth and build a Great City. Because the City or Camp of the Saints shall be broken into three parts and shall not rise again. For this time is spoken of in Rev. 17:8

> *8 And they that dwell on the earth shall wonder, <u>whose names</u> were <u>not written</u> in the <u>book of life</u> from the foundation of the world, when they <u>behold</u> the <u>beast</u> that <u>was</u>, and <u>is not</u>, and <u>yet is</u>.*

Because he comes in all lying wonders with a Great Knowledge and the strength therein. Therefore, lift up your eyes unto heaven and rejoice and you shall see the Lord of Glory in the clouds coming and is come when you see that which is coming upon the earth, even the Calamity. For who shall witness these things and what shall they see? Those of the world who can not believe, and they that have received the mark of the beast. They shall see a new beginning and a Great Restoration that will blind them from the truth. And the (2) Two Witnesses shall speak to both them and those of the (30) thirty fold and to bear witness to all that are on the earth in that day. This includes the High Ones and the Kings of the earth. For God has gathered them together for this cause . Now the (30) thirty fold shall be awakened by the works and testimony of these (2) two olive trees, and the (2) two candlesticks standing before the <u>God</u> of the <u>Earth</u>. For this time is written of in the book of Rev. 14:17 and it says:

14:17 And another angel came out of the temple which is in heaven, he also having a sharp sickle. And another Angel came out from the <u>altar</u>, which had <u>power</u>, over fire; and cried with a loud cry to him that had the sharp sickle, saying, thrust in thy sharp sickle, and gather the <u>clusters</u> of the <u>vine</u> of the earth; for her grapes are fully ripe. And the Angel <u>thrust in</u> his sickle into the earth, and gathered the <u>vine</u> of the earth, and cast it into the great wine press of the <u>wrath</u> of <u>God</u>. And *the wine press was trodden without the city. And blood came out of the wine press, even unto the horse bridles, by the space of a thousand and six hundred furlongs.* This being the harvest of the (30) thirty fold, which includes a number of the stranger who will be among them. For this is the strange work the Lord spoke of in Isa. 28:17 thru 28:22. *Judgment also will I lay to the line, and righteousness to the plummet: And the hail shall sweep away the refuge of lies, and the waters shall overflow the hiding place. And your covenant with <u>death</u> shall be <u>disannulled</u>, and your <u>agreement</u> with <u>hell</u> shall <u>not stand</u>: when the over flowing scourge shall pass through, then ye shall be trodden down by it. From the time that it goeth forth it shall take you: for morning by morning shall it pass over, by day and by night: and <u>it</u> shall be a <u>vexation</u> only to <u>understand</u> the <u>report</u>. For the bed is shorter than that a man can stretch himself on it: and the covering narrower than that he can wrap himself in it. For the Lord shall rise up as in mount Perazim, he shall be wroth as in the valley of Gibeon. That he may do his work, his <u>strange work</u>; and bring to pass his <u>Act</u>, his <u>strange Act</u>. Now therefore be ye not mockers, least your bands be made strong: for I have heard from the <u>Lord God</u> of <u>Hosts</u> a <u>consumption</u>, even <u>determined</u> upon the <u>whole earth</u>.* For in the last days a Great Knowledge comes forth, which will cause many to say: Who is like unto the beast? Who is able to make war with him? For they have become those who's <u>Names</u> are not <u>written</u> in the <u>book</u> of <u>life</u> of the <u>Lamb</u> slain from the foundation of the world. This is a knowledge from the High Ones, which is of old, Ancient of Days. To this cause many will ask: Who is Christ and from hence did he come ? Is he not of them, because of their power ? To them do I say: Hold fast to the truth which was given you before this one appears. For he is this one foretold who would come with all lying wonders. And would destroy wonderfully. Even so, the (2) Two Witnesses have power over him and because of him they shall bring forth plagues upon the earth. Those things which were poured out from the vials in <u>Spirit</u> shall be made manifest. And likewise the <u>Seals</u> and <u>Trumpets</u>, because each were done in <u>Spirit</u> and therefore not seen of men. To this cause the (2) Two Witnesses have the power to speak these things into being. And if any man should hurt them in like manner shall they die. Now the High Ones come from the seed of the Serpent, of whom we have never seen. But now has the time come that they shall be openly revealed to us. For we have been conditioned for this time over the last (20) twenty years. And we have been made ready that we should except them by reason of our increase of knowledge, because God from our beginning put enmity between the Serpent and the woman and between his seed and her seed. Therefore this One had to prepare us that we would receive him by reason of his Strength (Knowledge). Yet I tell you a Truth there is a portion of them that the Lord will receive unto Himself, because of a secret oath from Ancient of Days, which was broken. This oath was between Lucifer and a portion of the High Ones. For they remained silent until Enoch, the seventh from Adam did speak unto them. Then they, the High Ones did break out in one accord and sang unto the Lord.. The same shall be received of the Lord in these Last Days. Now concerning the seed of the Serpent, of whom we have not seen but have heard about. We know of them by the name of Extraterrestrial. They are of different origins as we are and have different appearances like-wise. There are some good and some not so good and others that are Evil in nature. Are we

not the same? Nevertheless, we have been separated from our collective history as mankind and lead to believe we are alone in this place. When the Truth comes, let it not take you from the Faith of God, our Lord Jesus Christ. For they would have you think differently. This will bring Great Tribulations which were never before nor will be again in this world. This One who comes brings a knowledge that will cast the Truth to the ground and make it appear as foolishness. Yet what is coming unto <u>all</u> in these Last Days, their knowledge can not stop it or change it. And <u>their</u> fear of it is why we are here and remain. For it was needful of them, that is to say, (High Ones) to find God of whom they lost by reason of this knowledge. Now Ancient of Days there are written many books concerning God Head and the things which must come to pass. And through mankind are certain things fulfilled. To this cause was and is our destiny. You must see this! It is to fulfill God's words that all these things have come to pass. Therefore believe in the <u>Faith</u> of <u>Jesus Christ</u> and not what is forth coming. Again I say, there is some good from this seed of the Serpent which comes, but not all, not even many, but some. Therefore look not by reason of your mind, but rather by Spirit and discernment and let the Holy Spirit guide you concerning them. For they are mentioned of in Isa.10:33 and Isa. 24:21 and Daniel 4:17 and again in Jer. 4:16 and also in Ezekiel 1:4 thru 1:28 and 10:9 thru 10:22. For they are called High Ones, Watchers and Living Creatures, according to these accounts. But they are known by many names. Even the Order of Melchizedek. Consider also the founders of Egypt and the people of China. For in their ancient history you will find evidence of them. For they are of old and go back to the Ancient of Days, even before the foundation of the earth. For God had set them in their places and gave them their part, but they would not hear in the time given and would not believe what they could not understand with their knowledge. For it required Faith in God to understand these things required of them. Nevertheless, these things are being accomplished in these Last Days.
Even so Oh Lord.

Amen ....

Now it is written in Rev. 13:5

> *5 And there was given unto him a mouth <u>Speaking</u> great things and <u>Blasphemies</u> and power was given unto <u>him</u> to continue forty and two months. And he opened his mouth in <u>Blasphemy</u> against God. <u>To Blaspheme</u> his <u>Name</u>, and his <u>Tabernacle</u>, and them that dwell in <u>heaven</u>.*

This <u>Blaspheme</u> spoken of here is concerning the history of mankind that is unknown to us. And the events that have taken place that we know not of. These things will turn some away from our Lord. Saying from hence did he come ? Who gave him his power ? For there is a Greater of man we know not of. And when we see him, will we also see the mark he has received. I speak of <u>them</u> and the seed of the Serpent together. And with them shall many be deceived. Even a host, for it is written in Rev. 13:13

13 And he doeth great wonders so that he maketh fire come down from heaven on the earth in the sight of men. And <u>deceiveth them</u> that dwell on the earth by the means of those miracles which he had power to do in the <u>sight</u> of the <u>beast</u>.

The beast is by reason of the knowledge which they bring and the image of the beast by reason of technology which comes from this knowledge. Yet I tell you a Truth, it is all lying wonders which blinded them in the Ancient of Days. And our ears have not heard nor our eyes seen these wonders and powers which they bring. And I say again, believe not on their power, because there is no wisdom within it. It requires not God in its being nor the love of God in its use. Therefore hold fast to the Faith of Christ Jesus whose Faith is beyond all understanding. For their knowledge came from the Evil One who changed the Truth which is God's cause for the Creation and made it a lie and because of this he (Satan) has deceived his own and yet there is a part of this seed which shall be saved and in this is the saying true, He shall be Glorious before His Ancients. Nevertheless, let not this coming knowledge or Ancient History cause you to stumble. Let your understanding be the Faith of Christ Jesus. And again, lean not on knowledge, but rather Faith and take hold of wisdom, which is trusting in God and His Word. Now this thing which is coming upon the earth of which the seed of the Serpent fears. It shall be seen coming by reason of many stars not giving their light. For it is the beginning of the end. To this cause do they now seek God, that is to say a part of them. For their Ancient writings speak of a <u>Man God</u> and they have looked toward us for Him. But they knew Him not in His coming. And now the time has come and is coming that the (2) Two Witnesses shall prophesy unto these High Ones and they (remnant) were affrighted and gave glory to the God of Heaven. And this is the last of those received unto the kingdom, even the (30) thirty fold. <u>And the nations were angry, and thy wrath is come</u>. Now let me repeat myself here and say more clearly the events that occur at this time. But in the days of the voice of the sixth angel, when he shall begin to sound, this is the coming and is come of the Angel of enlightenment (Rev. 18:1) and the time of the (2) Two Witnesses that they should begin to speak. And that their testimony shall bring in the Second Woe! Which is also the Rapture. And in this Calamity comes the fall of the Camp of the Saints. Then the coming of the Great City by reason of the Great Restoration. Now this is the time written of in Rev. 11:3

11:3 And I will give power unto my two witnesses, and they shall prophesy a thousand and two hundred and threescore days, <u>clothed</u> in <u>sackcloth</u>. 4 These are the two olive trees, and the two candlesticks <u>standing before</u> the <u>God</u> of the <u>earth</u>.

This also being the time of a Great One World Order by reason of the High Ones and the Kings of the earth. Remember what the Lord said about this One who will come in His own <u>Name</u> and the world will receive him and this is because of His Strength or Knowledge. Then comes Rev. 11:7

7 And when they shall have finished their testimony, the beast that ascendeth out of the bottomless pit shall make war against them, and shall overcome them, and kill them. And then Rev. 11:14

14 The second woe is past; and, behold, the third woe cometh quickly.

And this brings us again to Rev. 11:18

18 <u>And the nations were angry, and thy wrath is come</u>, and the time of the dead, that they should be judged, and that thou shouldest give reward unto thy servants the prophets, and to the saints, and them that fear thy name, small and great; and shouldest destroy them which destroy the earth.

Now to return and speak again about this knowledge that is forthcoming and the danger therein. This <u>Knowledge</u> and its <u>ability</u> to <u>break down Faith</u> is <u>liken</u> to the time and <u>doctrine</u> that the Pharisees and the Sadducees had in the time of Christ. Matt. 16:6

    6 Then Jesus said unto them, *Take heed and beware of the <u>leaven</u> of the <u>Pharisees</u> and of the <u>Sadducees</u>.*
    Then Matt. 16:11

11 How is it that ye do not understand that I spake it not to you concerning bread, that ye should beware of the leaven of the Pharisees and of the Sadducees?

And Matt. 16:12

12 Then understood they how that he bade them not beware of the leaven of bread, but of the <u>doctrine</u> of the <u>Pharisees</u> and of the <u>Sadducees</u>.

I say liken to, because in the time of Christ when He began revealing in parables the Truth and then other doctrine came to be used to deceive and cover what was given. So shall it be in the last days and the revealing of the Truth.. And as I said, this Knowledge and the doctrine that comes with it, even the technology, can and will cause many to stumble and fall away from Faith. I can not say it to much, because the danger of it is very real and powerful. And it came from a <u>Mighty One</u> in the <u>Beginning</u> of <u>Days</u>. Its power and strength is equal to whom it came from.. And remember this, the Evil One has the <u>power</u> and <u>strength</u> to <u>stand</u> before <u>All Mighty God</u> and <u>speak</u> these <u>Great Words</u>. For he has <u>understanding</u> of <u>Dark Sentences</u>. When I speak of All Mighty God, I'm speaking of this One from whose face the earth and the heaven fled away, and there was found no place for them. Rev. 20:11. For the Great White Thrown Judgment <u>is</u> God All Mighty. Now this anointed Cherub that Coverth, the same is he whom God in the Beginning of Days did anoint with <u>His Light</u> and the <u>Power</u> therein. What was given him in the Beginning was and is his for ever, even for ever and ever. But the increase thereof is God's for ever, even for ever and ever. Nevertheless, this One has Power even until the very end when he is cast "Alive" in the Lake of Fire. For he makes <u>War</u> and he <u>Exercises Authority</u> until the Great White Thrown Judgment. Therefore, know that he will and is having his Day and mostly his way, but not all. I say this because he has yet to make war with the (2) Two Witnesses. Even so he prepares himself for the time appointed. His Authority is spoken of in Daniel: 7:11

> *11 I beheld then because of the voice of the <u>great words</u> which the <u>horn spake</u>: I beheld even till the <u>beast</u> was slain, and his body <u>destroyed</u>, and given to the burning flame.*

And again Daniel: 7:15

> *15 I Daniel was grieved in my <u>spirit</u> in the midst of my <u>body</u>, and the visions of my head troubled me. 16 I came near unto one of them that stood by, and asked him the truth of all this. So he told me, and <u>made</u> me <u>know</u> the <u>interpretation</u> of the things.*

And again Daniel: 7:28

> *28 Hitherto is the end of the <u>matter</u>. As for me Daniel, my cogitations much troubled me, and my countenance changed in me: but I kept the matter in my <u>heart</u>.*

This saying that this man who is beloved of heaven and has the <u>gift</u> of <u>interpretation</u> and <u>visions</u> of <u>God</u>, could not understand nor could he <u>retain</u> the understanding when given to him, concerning these events that happen in the last days. And also the Beast and the Power and Authority of which he has in this time appointed. And the <u>Words</u> this <u>One spoke</u> brought much <u>confusion</u> because of its nature. I say these things so that you may <u>begin</u> to <u>understand</u> the complexity and the depth of this Knowledge and History that is coming upon the earth so that when it comes you will know of whom this report comes. For the Evil One would not foretell you of his deception, but rather use his subtle ways to blind your eyes and close your ears to hearing. I tell you now to do as Daniel did when these matters become confusing and troublesome to you. Hide them in your heart and let the Holy Spirit give you rest concerning them. It is impossible for you to understand the Truth of these matters using this Knowledge and History which comes. But what is impossible for man is very possible for God. Therefore I say unto you, wait upon the Lord and His Counsel before you seek to understand how all these things can be and how God could let such things come upon His Children. This much you can know and that is that God is always mindful of us and has created a place for us-ward that we shall have life eternal with Him. For this life which we have here in this place is not truly life, though it appears as such. For if it were life then we would also know <u>Him</u>, He who is the life giver. Yet we know Him not, nor His Name not even His cause. Therefore this is not life, but the way unto it. And the way unto it is to believe in the Son of God, even Son of Man, which is the promise of God come unto us. That we might enter there in and be made 'Alive' as He is. This being when the saying is true: Behold, I make all things New. Then shall come the New Heaven And the New Earth. And then shall the Sons Of God shine their light as the stars of Heaven. Consider then Daniel: 7:27

27 And the kingdom and dominion, and the greatness of the kingdom under the whole heaven, shall be given to the people of the saints of the most High, whose kingdom is an everlasting kingdom, and all dominions shall serve and obey him. And also Rev. 20:14

14 And death and hell were cast into the lake of fire. This is the second death. 15 And whosoever was not found written in the book of life was cast into the lake of fire. And Rev. 21:1

21:1 And I saw a new heaven and a new earth: for the first heaven and the first earth were passed away; and there was no more sea. And Rev. 21:3

3 And I heard a great voice out of heaven saying, Behold, the tabernacle of God is with men, and he will dwell with them, and they shall be his people, and God himself shall be with them, and be their God. 4 And God shall wipe away all tears from their eyes; and there shall be no more death, neither sorrow, nor crying, neither shall there be any more pain: for the former thing are passed away. Even so Oh Lord

Amen and Amen.......

To complete this summary I should say, the time before us is unlike any time that has ever been upon the Earth. The days are numbered, yet no man, not even the Angels in heaven know the day or hour that it should come. Only the Father, that is to say, the Holy Spirit, even the Spirit of Truth. Therefore, listen to no man who says he knows the day that it should come. But the Lord did say that if we will watch and be aware of the times and seasons we will see that day approach us, even as we can see the seasons of the year before they are fully come. In this manner are we made able to know that this time is before us so that we can rejoice in His coming. Nevertheless, this is a time where many hard things to understand shall come before us and try men's souls. And because of this, shall we find Great Tribulations to our Faith. To this cause is it possible that this day in its coming, could deceive us by reason of all the cares of this life and we would not see the day that it is fully come unto us. Because there is a Great Darkness, which appears as a Great Light, that should come before us in this day of days. How then can we count the number of days that we should know when the End has come before us. Daniel : 12:12

12. For Blessed is <u>he</u> that <u>waiteth</u>, and <u>cometh</u> to the <u>thousand three hundred and five and thirty days</u>.

This speaking of the time after the Rapture and the building of the Great City like no other before it. And the time just before the <u>final visitation</u> of <u>God</u>. Which is the last day. The number of days is given to be <u>45</u>, but not the day that you should start counting. Therefore, no one knows the day nor the hour, but it is now given unto man to know the season, if you will watch and discern by reason of the spirit. For all these things must come, but only those with some understanding will look in spirit and know in its coming. Even so Oh Lord.

Amen and Amen.......

~Revalation Prophecies~

Writings of a Prophet / 1982
(Before Hand)

The following in this testament was written in nineteen eighty two and eighty three (1982-83). Then the Lord said:

Seal up this testament for many days and go and live the days which I have added unto you, until I return and finish the work which I have given you. For it will be in your generation that I will accomplish the works there in. And in that day shall they know that I have spoken these words unto you...

Amen and Amen......

P.S.

** *In the time of the writings that follow, there were things that were not yet revealed and to that cause you will notice an expansion on the subject on page 19 thru 22, (Seals) which was added on to explain more clearly the events and their meanings as well as the* <u>hidden wisdom</u>, *which* <u>God ordained</u> *before the world and to our glory, that is to say His Children, which is spoken of in Cor. 2:7. Which is speaking of before the foundation of the world. The rest of the text is as it was written in that day.*

~Revelation Prophecies~

~Holy Spirit~

Oh Holy Spirit, Glory is Your Great Power Most High is Your Name, and Presence is Your Being Are You not with us in this day.

Howbeit, is there any among men, that can not hear Your Truthful walking, In this the cool of the evening, of the Lord's Great Day.

Woe is it of the Darkness of this that day. For the Night thereof, they shall see Great Sorrows and the Truth which was the Light therein, it shall surly be gone away.

For man shall not kill himself, but only hurt. It is Fate that will destroy him, it is the Soul that has been saved.

And the spirit You can find, but first you must perceive it, for it lies within the walls of peace of mind.

For the Truth is still yet with you, put down offense, oh hear the heart of Truth if you can.

To each man it comes in the choosing, from this One who is within. For it is All who shall see it. It is the weeping and wailing that is outside.

When shall we be able to at last put offense down. It is the Truth Only, who was able and He showed us that state of mind. It is God the Father who made All things, even Fate, not the man in front or behind.

Therefore trust Him, He has revenge on those that hurt you with their words and with their hands. Don't pick up offense, and if you should find it in your heart or even your hand.

Pick up this Truth, though it may seem heavy, knowing offense can not abide. For it is Truth only which can bear it, It is impossible for the man.

For you are not able to carry him. He will destroy you with his way. You not knowing he is not you, he himself becomes your ways.

Where then are you ? How can you stand ? When offense has become your only eye. There is no rest in your being, Only the needs of the offense shall you find.

The cost of offense is one spirit made many, A house divided, How can it stand ? Yet there is One who is among you, He is meek, put your trust in His restful Hand.

For God made man to be a peaceful spirit, not an offensive one, now is the time to understand. Know then what hurts you, it is the Spirit that Quickens, even as it is in man.

Judge not your brother, know the Truth, it is not he who raises his hand. If you know this is so, then offense can not hold you by your thoughts or even your hands.

Know the time is, that this season is upon us and arm yourself with Truth or become as Death in offense and Revenge.

For they have come out unto you, in the mind as in the land. For even Nature will go against you, but know theTruth.God is Nigh! He is at hand !

It will appear that your neighbor hurts you, but forgive him when you can believe the Truth. For your nearest neighbor is in your family, but yet as Nature, likewise Time, he must erupt too.

Know the season, look about you, behold the Spirit of Truth cries, God the Father has come unto you, he is Spirit. Put on this state of mind.

Know what has come unto you, know also just before Night, in the midst of the evening, this then becomes the Twilight. Take then this Twilight unto you, hold it fast into the Night. It will not fail you nor forsake you, God's Glory is His Might.

Think not that this Night will leave you, but that it is you that must leave it. For the spirit of offense is the Night come unto you and the Spirit of Truth that shall take you into Light.

Hear now the Truth while you are yet able, that the Earth must become a Fire. For it is the given Word of our Heavenly Father. It is the Night that is the Liar.

Oh fathers, love your son, even when he can not you, it is the Spirit of Love that shall save him, even likewise unto you.

Mother, daughter, sister, brother, even neighbor. it remains the same. It is Love that takes you Home, and offense that will make you stay.

Know then what seeks to hurt you, that you might put it down, when it picks you up. Put not your Faith in the world around you, but rather in this Truth you must abide.

In this Truth you'll find Forgiveness has the Power over offense, and be not fearful, but yet trembling, for the Lord has done the rest.

For we are yet blind and see not this Truth, it has been accomplished. And the Great weight becomes the lesser, It is the Father's Grace that bears the weight.

In this Twilight learn old and new Praises, they are sung in the New Most High. For they are the Lord and the Holy Father, There is No One else who are able to abide.

"Behold We Create a New" is the cry of One who is Most Greater than I. Yet I tell you, I've always been with Him, even before they were One, It is I.

Yet know we're together, He is Glorious in the sight of His Perfect Light. For it is Nigh, He comes out of hiding as the Twilight before the Night.

Alleluia ! God, Himself is come unto you. Forever More and More

Amen and Amen....

k-2

~Seven Keys~

1) <u>Love</u>: Love thy God (Heavenly Father) with all thy Heart and all thy Soul and with all thy Mind, for He so Loved the world (His children), He gave His only begotten Son, so that we may also be His Sons.

2) <u>Faith</u>: (believing) For if you have Faith the size of a mustard seed; All things are possible. For Faith is total and consuming, like that of Love, one holding onto the other.

3) <u>Patience</u>: For patience is the door to wisdom and understanding like that of the Saints. For patience is to Faith as Faith is to Love. One holding onto the other. Therefore patience is a test to Faith, as Faith is to Love. One making the other stronger.

4) <u>Truth</u>: Be true to thyself and you shall learn thyself. For if you can not speak Truth to yourself, you can not speak Truth to your Father, which is within you. <u>Ask</u> through Love and Faith and you shall receive patience; <u>Seek</u> with patience and you shall find Truth; <u>Knock</u> and you shall stand within (The Holy Place) and wisdom and understanding shall be yours.

5) <u>Mercy</u>: (Forgiveness) For as your Father in Heaven forgives you, therefore you must forgive others. He that created you and All things also created others. He who gives Mercy shall Receive it also. If you can't find mercy for others. How then can it be found for you also.

6) <u>Give</u>: (Charity) For it is more Blessed to give then receive. As your Father in Heaven gives unto you, so also should you give unto others. He who gives to them that are of true need, shall receive of the Father. They that give only to receive will find no increase in their joy.

7) <u>Love</u>: Love thy neighbor as thy should Love thyself. For the Last is liken to the First. If you Love not your neighbor as yourself, you then therefore are not able to Love your Heavenly Father which is within you. For if you can not Love that

which you are able to see, then therefore how will you be able to Love that which you can not see (Your Heavenly Father) that is within you. Be "Humble" and do unto others as you would have them do unto you. Love thy neighbor, even if he hates you. For if he hates you, he shall inherit his own hatred. Love and you shall have your Heavenly Father's Love.

~ Prayer ~

Oh Praise thee Lord God for thou hast not forsaken us. Yea, You speak unto the Heart continually and show Mercy and Compassion unto us that we might hear this Heart that thou speakest to.

Oh Praise thee Son of God, for it is by You and through You that we might All be Sons of God.

Oh Praise thee Holy Ghost, for thou art the Spirit of Truth, dwelling within us guiding, protecting and comforting, save he that might hear thee.

Oh Praise thee Almighty God, for thou art indeed the Father, the Son, the Holy Ghost.

Amen....

Father, that I might Praise thee, Yet there is but One Good. And if I should Praise thee, then Hallelujah, for thou then art with us. Even so Father

Amen and Amen.....

If any man should desire to know the Long-suffering of the Lord God, for they are His Friends. Let this man write deeply into his mind, which is to say, his part of his Spiritual Heart, this prayer, so that the times and the seasons of his life will not cover it nor divide the Light thereof nor part it from his vision of his life. Therefore the patience and Faith of the Saints will teach him. Even so oh Lord.

Amen and Amen......

Glory to God and His Christ, for whom the prophets and the Saints came forth unto the earth. Let every man great and small, free and in bondage who can see his own sin and know that he and his forefathers share the same iniquities and know he himself is not worthy of God's forgiveness. Utter this prayer of Truth with the Power of God's Grace and Love of God's Son

Amen...

Lord of my Lord, forgive me, for I am a sinner. Even now as I pray unto you, my sins and iniquities are Great. Yet surely You Love us All, for You have given us many things. Thy Spirit of Truth, which is Life and the material things we need, let us Glorify thee. Yet I am not worthy, for You have put Your Love in my Heart, Soul and Mind, that I might love thee. For Bless it be the Father, He gave of Himself the Only Begotten Son, so that not all the world should perish. Bless it be the Son, for He is of the Father and likewise has given of Himself. Bless it be the Holy Ghost, for He is of the Son and to the Father Most Sacred and Holy, even so, He has been given unto us. Bless it be Almighty God, for He is the Father, the Son, the Holy Ghost.

Amen.......

Father who art in Heaven, Hallowed be thy Name. Thy Kingdom has begun, thy Will is done on earth as it is in Heaven. For thou hast given us each day our daily needs and forgave us our trespasses, even as we forgive those who trespass against us. Leading us not into temptation, but has delivered us from Evil. For thine art the Kingdom, the Power and the Glory. Forever and ever.

Amen...

Faith, indeed it is the substance of things hoped for, the evidence of things not seen. Therefore if a man should believe in the walking with God though he receive not material things the greater is the faith that he walks in. Even as it was of old times. For God is the author and worker of faith thereby walking with any man who is made able to believe in the works of God through Christ Jesus though he may not receive of material things and if he should, let him then give even as it was given unto him. And should he receive of Heavenly things, let him then give the more to those who have need of God and of Truth. For God desires to give His Kingdom unto His children to this cause was each created, heaven and earth. Will it <u>not</u> be fulfilled? God forbid! For there is this Kingdom (the way it has been and is) which must end and the Kingdom to come (the way it will be for ever more) which is the promise fulfilled. For as the prophets received the promise and yet what man witnessed it save one Jesus, Son of Man, the Lord Christ. For He said, Abraham saw it and was glad. And also namely this; what a man believes (sees) in his heart the same will be done. If he should see in his heart to kill his neighbor he then is guilty of it. And if he should not turn from his ways, he then is destined to do it and it shall surely be done. This is the law, even as it is given concerning lust, hatred, deceitfulness and all manner of evil. For if you meditate of these things so then do they become you. But likewise is it true to meditate all manner of good things namely this; Love, Forgiveness, Compassion, considering others even as yourself. Be Slow to Anger and Quick to forgive and when someone hurts you remember this; if you desire the same unto him then his hurt to you is justified and therefore measured back unto you. Know this also, if you rather pray for those who hurt you then your Love for them is justified and measured back unto you by the Heavenly Father Himself. Therefore know the Truth as it was given unto you by the Lord Jesus: Love your enemies and pray for those who use and persecute you and Great is your reward in Heaven. Those who are able to walk in this Faith the same receive not by merit but rather Faith and to this cause their Greatness remains in Heaven where it can not be stolen nor changed neither can it be harmed, even so Oh Holy One

Amen...

Nevertheless the Promise unto the Prophets was received indeed, but not seen of men. Yet in Faith is he made able to see it therefore knowing this law is true: He to whom much is given, much is required and to whom little is given, little is required. Yea, there is a greater and lesser of each. This being true in both material and spiritual things (Wealth). And there is a greater and lesser in each of these. That is to say he who gives and he who gives not, yet says he gives. First let me explain: For God has allowed <u>hunger</u> and <u>death</u> come upon the lands that each man shall enter into his own Judgment and receive of his own works. He to whom much is given even to he to whom little is given. For each have a part. Now to show of each of these: He to whom much is given in the wealth of the lands has yet a need for where there is wealth (riches) there is also a danger of Blindness (vanity, vanity all is vanity) to this cause the cries of those in need of these things must be brought to the hearts of those to whom much is given, even by those to whom little is given in the wealth of the lands. As to touching this part or side of this law understand the lesser and greater of it in this manner: He who received much and is the greater,

1

let him give even as it is given unto him. In the Name of (Happiness) of the Lord, which by His Power was it allowed. And the lesser shall give little or none because of the hardening of his heart. For the greater shall Glorify God in the giving and not himself. And the lesser who gives little shall glorify himself by saying in his heart and thereby his mouth shall also speak it and say; by God's help I have given or I have helped God do His Good Works. For which is easier to say, yet both are untrue because there is but One who is Good, The Heavenly Father, and if any good works are found in your hand, let it be known unto you, even as unto the Just that it is the Lord passing through him and Glorify the same. For what man has done a good work truly? There is None! Yet good works are found in his hand. Know then the truth; God is the doer of All Good Works and man being the image is seen as the doer but truly only the shadow and not the very works. To this cause did our Lord Christ Jesus say for a man to humble himself and he shall be lifted up by the Holy Spirit and shall witness the good works found in himself and give God and His Christ the glory and the man shall be found with no unrighteousness in him. But if a man should see some good in himself he will feel he only needs a little help of God or even worse he may believe that God can do nothing without the help of some man such as himself. This being a man who gives nothing, yet says in himself that he has given. And he who may see some good in himself, the same shall give little because he hears in himself that God shall help him to give not knowing that it is God who gives unto him as well as through him. And because he does not understand this Truth he shall desire honor of men for the works found in his hand and this will make the gift little no matter how much he should give. For that which a man has in himself alone is little, even as a shadow and that which is added unto him shall make him either an image of good or evil. For if the man sees his Accomplishment he then can not see God's Works and he will not honor God, but shall dishonor himself with self glory and evil is the image thereof. Yet if the man should see the works of God in himself and humble himself before God and man, the works done in him shall be increased the more and good is the image thereof. Yea, this which is found in a man alone is faith and in itself is only little. Yet if applied unto the works of God it becomes a Great Source of Light. But likewise if applied unto the works of men it becomes a Great Source of Darkness. For man is fallen and remembers not the God of Light. This in itself leaves him in Darkness. Now that we have touched the Material things given unto a man, let us speak concerning Spiritual things, and the lesser and greater that such a man might give. He to whom much is given and is the greater shall give the more for it shall be continually added unto him and he will give God all the Glory. For God is the increase. And many shall receive of this greater one. Whether it be the gift of Healing or whether it be words of knowledge or the working of miracles or the understanding of or speaking of Prophecy whether it be words of Wisdom or Discerning of Spirits or tongues or interpretation of tongues, even faith or increase of faith. For what a man has in himself alone is little, yet even that was a gift from the beginning. And if he should honor the giver will it not be increased and if he should dishonor the giver will it not decrease? Nevertheless, all of these gifts are of the self same Spirit and He gives to every man severally as He will. This being the Works of God the Holy Spirit. Even so Father,

Amen.....

2

Now the lesser man shall take of these gifts and hide it in himself by reason of self glory. And give not God the Praise. For he will say in his heart that he has earned this gift by reason of his works or give God some of the Glory and say in himself that because God has given him this gift that he himself is worthy of it. And by so doing shall loose even that which he has and his portion shall become that of the unbelievers and the last state of the man is worse then the first. For in his beginning he was given little. Yet if he should do well, it will surely wax great before him and if he should dishonor this gift it shall become as nothing. For all that he shall have is his own self glory and this shall be his only reward. This being a shadow which shall surely fade away. For men do honor such a glory for a small space of time then they will require even more from such a man then he is able in himself to deliver and to this cause shall they remove him out of the way and he will be consumed in their fire and here is the saying true: For unto whomsoever much is given, of him shall be much required: and to whom men have committed much, of him they will ask the more. And again; For he that hath, to him shall be given: And he that hath not, from him shall be taken even that which he hath. Yea, God is the giver of every good gift and the children of light perfect Praise unto Him, even so Oh Holy One Amen..... Now that we have considered the greater and lesser of a man who has received of Spiritual things and of material things; this brings us back to that which God has allowed to come upon the earth. That is to say death and hunger and famine. For if these things exist, even as they do, why and to what cause are they? There are those who say it is their Karma from another life. Even as the disciples had asked Jesus concerning a man <u>born blind. Whether the blind man had sinned</u> or his <u>father</u> before him. And Jesus answered saying; this man has not sinned, nor his father, but that he was a manifestation of God. Therefore know and understand that there are those who receive little in spiritual things such as this blind man who knew not in himself the Lord, yet was sent unto the world in the Lords coming not because of sin, but by reason of God's works. That is to say, a manifestation of God. What then is the understanding? To whom much is given, much is required and to whom little is given, little is required. This being true for Spiritual things even as material things. For this blind man had little in material things because he was a beggar and also little in spiritual things, because he knew not his Lord, yet the prophet John the Baptist knew his Lord because he was given much Spiritually and much was required of him, even his life. Nevertheless, he received even more, which is true <u>Life Everlasting</u>. This a man is not able to see with his eyes of flesh, but with your ear are you able to see that which was given him upon the earth. For the Lord Himself gave testimony of this (man) prophet, that there was not a Greater prophet born of a woman's womb than he and also he was given among men to prepare the Way of the Lord. Yea, God has honored this man Greatly before His Angels as well as before men. Such an honor comes from God "Only". Indeed this man received much and even more was given unto him. Even so Father

Amen and Amen......

And what of the blind man! If he was given little in material and spiritual things, what is there to learn of him? The little given in material things was his very flesh, which kept him in the midst of his needs. And the little given in spiritual things was his faith. And to this cause when the Lord came before him and anointed his eyes with clay he did follow his instructions so that he might receive his sight and in receiving his sight he also desired to know his Lord which was an increase of the spiritual things given him. And as to the poor of the world that know not the Lord in their mind, but in their heart is hidden the truth, the same are manifestations of God. Nay, you can not tell one from the other for outwardly they look the same as those which have had taken away that which they have. Know this, it is not for us to Judge one another, but rather witness the very works of God. There are those that say and speak against the things that happen in the world and yet when they are made able to do something to help they themselves turn away. As it was said before; God has Allowed these things to happen upon the Earth so that each man shall surely enter into his own works. Be careful therefore what you speak and what you measure unto others and yourselves. For it shall truly be measured back unto you again. As to the poor in spirit, the Lord himself said theirs is the Kingdom of God, which is truly, truly much. And those poor in material things the same receive in the spiritual and as they do so shall it be done unto them. That is to say, if he has little in the wealth of the land he then either has great need and dwells in the midst of his needs, which means that he is a manifestation of God and God's works shall be done unto him for the sake of others or he is full in Spirit and gives Joy unto those who are able to receive it. If he dwells in the midst of his needs he then stands with those which God shall give much in the Kingdom of God before His Holy Angels. Even so Oh Lord

Amen and Amen......

And again he who has much in material things should give even as it is given him and if he should not, then he has received his reward in <u>Death</u> and shall not know <u>Life</u>, but shall hold unto the things which he has and not help those who are in need of such things. And to this cause he perceives that he needs nothing and he will hold on to these things even until they fade away. To this cause did our Lord say; It is easier for a camel to go through the eye of a needle then for a rich man to enter into the Kingdom of Heaven. But what is impossible for man is possible for God. Therefore He will perform these works in us using His time. For many who are rich in the things of this world will put their trust in these things and will not handle the things of Life but will hold fast to the things that are dead and perceive themselves living and Alive. Yet there are those who have received riches of the world that they might know this Truth and Abide. Therefore know and understand that one can not outwardly see which of these men might stand before him and he should not Judge, but witness only and in doing so he shall see the end works of this one and know by his fruits and as you can see, there was no need for Judgment, but only to witness for the Lord's Judgment is True. As He said: There is <u>not one good man, no not one</u>, but there are <u>Just</u> men made perfect in Christ Jesus and to this cause they do <u>give God All</u> the <u>Glory</u>, because they are born again in Spirit *and He is their perfection. And it is His good works seen in them and to this cause do they give Him all the glory by giving their testimony before men and by praising God openly. Even so Holy Father*

Amen.......

So if the Lord should do His good works in us and we give Him the glory and the honor, then He has also given us wisdom and our blessings are made manifest and magnified unto us. For what a man has in himself is little, even a measure of faith. But God desires to increase our blessings and to restore us unto Himself.

Amen.......

My friends, this is the true saying of God. Seek first the Kingdom of God and the rest shall be added unto you. The meaning of this saying is this: First find and settle within yourself that God truly was, is and will be. Which is only to say, He has His purpose, and will and has succeeded in it, and that you are a part of that purpose and that success. Seek always to reflect His ways; Slow to anger, quick to Forgive, continually loving to one another. To do these things are truly worshipping the Lord. To trust Him is to Not Judge One Another, but rather witness only. This is to say, live in the manner of these His ways. And let this One who Judges be Judged of Himself. For he who Judges shall truly be Judged of his own Judgment. And if that Judgment is false (to be not so) then he himself shall become the same. Where then is he, and what is his name? Look then about you and come out of his place and be not of his name. Know then the Truth. The Lord God has created All things, even this One who is Evil. As it is written in Isaiah 45:5: I am the Lord, and there is none else, there is no God beside me: I girded thee, though thou hast not known me: 6 That they may know from the rising of the sun, and from the west, that there is none beside me. I am the Lord, and there is none else. 7 I form the light, and create darkness: I make peace, and create evil: I the Lord do all these things. Indeed, all things, came forth from God Himself. Therefore He knowing all things, has purged Himself. He has taken a part of Himself and cast it off. He knowing all things has done this for our sake. Therefore, know this Truth. Be then like-minded; Cast from you the same. He, Himself, has made it "possible". Put on The "New Creature", that He has made (created). This is to say put on "Christ". Be like-minded. This can and has been done in the Name of the Lord Christ. I, even I, cry unto you that you might hear these words, for they are "True Spirit". Find place in you for this "Spirit". It is for your sake it has come. It is for man's sake that it cries in this the last hour of Redemption. Hear this Truth and Abide. Because of this spirit of offense and the accuser you must hear this "Truth" to be saved. This Evil One will have you to Judge and accuse one another. Therefore, divide him by this means; If you must Judge, then Judge yourself only and in this Judgment know that you are a sinner, and that you are guilty of "All" sin. Find yourself "not clean". Let the remaining days of your life be in this "Truth" and God shall raise you up into His Righteousness and you will be found "clean". Made white in His Glory. Accuse not one another, and seek not your own glory. This is to say, let not this

One of Evil *persuade* you to desire your own *credits* of *accomplishment*. That is indeed to say, have *praise* of *men*. For men honor their own kind. Likewise is it of God. For *only God* "hears" *Gods'* *Word*. Did not our Lord Christ say to this certain man; Why do you call me good? There is but "One" who is good: My Father in Heaven! Know this "Truth" in this the Last hour and be not deceived. In this "Truth" given; you shall "possess" your own souls; This is to say, choose "Light" or "Darkness", for your eternal consciousness. What can *you believe*? Know this, without this "Truth" you can lose your soul. What is impossible with man is possible for God. Therefore, know and trust He has done it. To this cause I, even I, a sinner beseech you to consider this which is written in Isaiah 64:6 But we are all as an *unclean thing*, and *all* *our* *righteousness* are as *filthy rags*; and *we all* do *fade* as a *leaf*; and *our iniquities*, like the wind, have *taken us away*. 7 And there is *none* that *calleth* upon *thy name*, that *stirreth up himself* to take *hold* of *thee*: for *thou* hast *hid* thy *face from us*, and *hast consumed us*, because of *our iniquities*. 8 But *now*, O *Lord*, thou art *our* *Father*; *we are* the *clay*, and *thou* *our* *potter*; and *we all are* the *work* of *thy hand*. So it is written, is it not so? Therefore I, even I of *great Iniquities*, cry unto the *earth* and *all* of its *inhabitancy*. "Receive" onto *you* this "Contrite Spirit", and *hold fast* onto this "Truth". For "He" is *The Spirit of Truth*. Even so Father, it Is "Your Glory", and "Your Being" and your Grace toward us... Hallelujah!

Amen and Amen.......

So if we will seek His Kingdom first, then He will add His Grace to us-ward and all things that we desire in our hearts He shall give us, because in seeking Him first we will learn from His Goodness and come to know the things of Life and our desires will turn toward Him because we can taste of His Love for us and come to know His Joy and Peace. For what man is worthy unto God and who is like Him? There is none, but God has made us that *He* should *dwell* within us. Therefore, *He* has made a way that we might receive *Him worthily*. And if we should receive *Him*, then we shall become like *Him*. To this cause are we *born* *again* and made a "New Creature". Because He cleans the inside so that the outside might be clean also. Let this be your understanding and it will comfort you while He the Lord performs a mighty work in you and you truly become a "New Creature" before *God* and *men*. Because others who know you and see the works of God in you become witnesses by reason of the works and then both God and His works are glorified, and men are made able to see, hear and understand the Being of God. Even so Oh Lord it is your good pleasure to restore us unto your Being.

Amen........

Spirit of Truth, thou art forever with us. Let us rejoice in thy presence of being. Restore unto us your simplicity of creation, that we might have remembrance of the things that remain. For God the Father created *All* *Things* *Spirit* by the *Power* of *His Will*, which is His Being. Everything which was, is and will be, must first be spirit then if God desired (allowed) it becomes manifested. Even as it is written in Genesis 2:5 And every plant of the field *before it was in the earth*, and every herb of the field *before it grew*: for the Lord God had not caused it to rain upon the earth, and there was not a man to till the ground This is only to say, He created it *First Spirit*. All things that are manifested (physical) are because there is a spirit representation to make it so. Yet there are spirits which have no material being. What then is the law that applies to them and to material things? For there must be a law of Creation that will apply to both, if it is a true law. For each is a state of being and should reflect one another. This law of creation is to put it simply, as this: All spirits must reflect its being; either by state of physical manifestation or by state of physical laws themselves. That is to say, what we foolishly call energy. For example; A magnetic field has no physical substance, yet it does exist. Some use the term "lines of force". The best example I could give, is the forces that hold the planets and all the heavenly bodies in place and even cause the seasons to occur. Consider this, Jesus said that God has put His Power (Spirit) into the "Times and Seasons". Now we know that God is spirit and we know that none of us can see Him. Are you beginning to see this True Law, and how it has been applied to the visible and the invisible? Let me explain, as it is written: God made man an image of Himself. As we said earlier, God is spirit and we are an image of Him. Therefore, our physical manifestation or body is an image of our spirit, which is part of God and as all things; came forth out of God. Please don't misunderstand this saying. We did not come directly out of God, but rather we came out of that which came forth from God. Therefore spirit will take one of (3) three states. Either a physical state, or an energy field state or it becomes a state of time and space. As it should be possible for you to see. All things visible and invisible of the creation will fit in one of these three states. Even the universe itself, which is all three. Knowing this you should also know that heavenly bodies such as Earth is a *Living Thing*. A Gem of the Heavens. And upon it there is of course Living things. Even as your body is a living thing and has living things upon it. For there are many levels of heaven. From the least to the great. These levels have (2) two sides. One by reason of "*Purpose*" and the other by reason of "*Will*". To say by reason of "*purpose*" means it exists not for itself, but to support another form of Life. To say by reason of "Will" means it chooses whether to remain the same or change its state of being or awareness and therefore itself. There is yet a third form to consider and that is the elements themselves. Which are not alive as we perceive it, but is as all things "Spirit". All Spirit coming from God and God being Alive. Therefore, even the elements which are by reason of *constant* have life in God, but not in itself. To say *constant* means no form of spirit can manifest without its presence, save God Alone. God being constant and the elements likewise. For the elements can not be broken down to a lesser state and therefore become the building blocks of all physical things that were, that are and that will be. The matter of what elements are together is determined by time and space, and the *purpose* and/ or *will* of said Spirit. For spirit is greater and manifestation the lesser of the Being State. And all spirit being created by God and each shall have its due season. This is only to say that God has His purpose for "*everything*" He creates. As it is written: For *thou* hast *created all things*, and *for thy pleasure they are* and *were created*. Now the Spirit is greater then the manifestation because God Himself has touched the Spirit to create it and the manifestation is

7

by reason of the spirit or to say a reflection of said spirit. For as God created each part, He looked and saw that it was "good". This saying that God being the "Sum" was able to know if that which He made was able to serve and accomplish His purpose. Even before it was, which is to say spirit not yet in its season. To this cause did man perceive evolution against Creation. Not knowing the mystery of the times and seasons and thereby believing over time things did evolve from its beginning. Not knowing that everything in its due season will manifest and/or change form. For all things were in the beginning, even Christ, likewise in its end. For the First Resurrection Glorified the Son and the Second Resurrection shall glorify God the Father. For this reason there were (12) twelve Thrones of Judgment for the First Resurrection and (1) Throne of Judgment for the Second. The (12) twelve being of the Son who is in the Father and the One being God the Father and there is none who stand beside Him. Therefore, God shall receive all that was given, which is in the Son, unto Himself and that which He, Himself has given unto its place (Lake of Fire). Then shall He create a new. For that which God cast from Himself, must be sacrificed or else it was not given. Yet it must have a purpose if it was created and therefore a spirit. For it too must exist because God said it would and it being spirit must abide in the laws of creation. With this understanding of these laws you can begin to see how God can use this spirit (Lake of Fire) in the New Creation and have this Great Gap between it and the Everlasting Kingdom. The laws I speak of are the states of being (Spirit) and how All coexist and the ways God has, is, and will be creating the Everlasting Kingdom. The laws God used in the beginning, have not failed Him nor dishonored Him. For He has used them to Judge Himself and has found the Judgment Good. If not, then the Son would not have come. And because He did, then the last day must come likewise. For the Powers of Heaven will be shaken and God the Father will take what remains and create a new and Everlasting Kingdom that will not pass away. For as it was in the beginning, so shall it be in its end. That is to say Spirit. If we take one of these laws of creation and apply it to a manifestation which we call a star or sun, we will begin to understand what I speak of. The physical state of the sun is such that the very mass of it is being broken down to a lesser state. To say in simple terms, it is being burned or changing state of form. Now the manifestation is a reflection of its spirit. Therefore, this Heavenly body is not stable nor is its spirit at any level of rest. Now we know that each star or sun has its number of days being a sun and then it will burn out or Nova. When this occurs (burn out) the star or sun will loose most of its physical size, but its Gravitational Field remains the same. This is to say that the spirit or true substance of this Heavenly body is changing form. For this reason the physical size has decreased, but the gravitational field has not. The physical manifestation. (one form of spirit) changing to energy and physical laws (another form of spirit) showing or reflecting that the spirit of this Heavenly body is yet present and continuing to be. Now if this star or sun should Nova. Then it is changing to the form of (time and space) and the Gravitational Field may no longer exist. And if not, then gases and dust will be all that remains, which states that this heavenly body has converted mostly to the form of time and space. Now if the gravitational field still exist, then this heavenly body has changed to the form of energy and physical laws. For what God has *made it shall always be. And He shall put "each" in its "place", Forever and Ever. For should God make that which has not purpose, He has erred.. Now in the beginning God created All things and looked and saw that it was good (had purpose). He has not erred . It is man's perception that has erred. And even that has God a purpose for. And we shall witness it, and with wonder shall it be revealed unto our remembrance. For man has fallen and remembers not the God of Light. Therefore his God is darkness and all the <u>unknown</u> that is in <u>him</u>, which is the face of the Deep. To this cause do I say man's perception has erred, because man's mind is his master and the God of Darkness has made his seat the same. Indeed, Satan has desired us and has walked in us and we know him not, even though we have his many faces upon us and do the many works that he has given us to do. And the things that we would trust in are not the things that will help us find our way back into the Light. But praise be unto God the Son for He has made a way that we can return unto Him, even to Himself. And to this cause do I say: Praise be onto God the Holy Spirit for he is with us this day and we are made able to receive of the Lord in these last days, even in the midst of the power of Darkness in the night of this day.*

Amen....

And here is the understanding and the patience and Faith of the Saints, that we should understand in due season. We are all equal to one another, the just and the unjust. For it is written, the Lord God lets it rain on the just and the unjust equally. For each is needed unto the Mystery of the Creation of God. That which the Lord God does and allows to be, is good indeed, even if it is beyond our understanding. The Lord God, His Name is <u>All</u>, is the Father of all of the creation. The visible and the invisible. That which has substance and that which has not. (That which was, but is not, yet is). We are that which has not substance though it seems so. And spirit is that which has substance, though it seems to have not. For we are not able to see spirit unless it is revealed unto us. For this reason we must look not only outside of us, (the world and all around us) where substance appears to be, but also look within where true substance, indeed is. That is to say, where God is. For Jesus said; The Kingdom of God is within. The Lord Jesus also said; That we are to watch, even until He returns. This means the outside as well as within. For this reason we are made "witnesses" and not Judges. As Jesus said; Judge not and you will not be Judged. For if you "<u>witness</u>" only, then <u>only</u> your "<u>testimony</u>" is required of <u>you</u>, but if <u>you</u> Judge, it <u>must</u> be <u>Judged onto you</u>.This is the "Law of Creation" and how will you defy it. It is not possible! For God is Greater then All. To refer back to the just and the unjust is only to say, he that believes and he that believes not. This is also to say the Mystery of God. Howbeit, that God who created all things has allowed the unjust, <u>unbeliever </u>to be? Consider this, In the beginning God created heaven and earth and in heaven, this One (who is called Satan and the Devil) came unto the throne of God, and <u>Him</u> who sets upon it, and believes Him not and accused Him of His Authority. This then began the Mystery of God. For God has always been. It is written that God took "nothing" and created All things. For with each of us is that which is, and that which is not. And we know not one from the other, the spirit and the consciousness (the substance and the non substance). For your mind (consciousness) perceives that your body (flesh) is your substance. Yet your true self is not body, but spirit. For your body is just an image of your spirit. For the Lord God created man an _image_ of Himself, and your spirit draws life from God's Power and Grace. Yet your consciousness being not body, is not "true spirit", for it knows not where it is, nor remembers where it is from. For your "true spirit" (soul) stands before God, least there would be no life in you at all. As Jesus said, Your angel (true spirit) stands before the face of My Heavenly Father in Heaven, even as Son of Man is in heaven. Howbeit that Jesus (Son of Man) while yet in the world (flesh) could be in heaven also? Howbeit that Jesus said that as He sees the Father do, He does likewise, if He was yet in the world? Even as David when he said, The Lord of my Lord said, sit thou on my right hand until I make thy enemies thy footstool. This is to say, "In the Spirit". And indeed, "true spirit" stands before God and draws Life from Him alone. For God desires to dwell with man, but _man is not_. For Adam is the Father of all flesh, even as it is written. But Adam transgressed against God. For the Lord God said unto Adam, if you do this which I have commanded you not to do, you will surely die. My Beloved, the Lord God is not a liar. Adam indeed died when he was cast from the "presence" of God. Howbeit, that you and me are alive if Adam is our father? For Adam's children (as we are all his children) are born in death, we know not the Lord God, but desire to know Him. This is the inheritance from Adam. Let me give unto you as it is given unto me. Without God you are _dead_. If you know not God nor His Face, you are indeed dead! What man among you has seen the Lord's Face? There is none. For Moses gave us Truth. No man can stand before the Lord or look upon His Face. Only God's Glory can look upon His Face. It is God's Mercy and Grace that Adam had children and it is in this understanding when Jesus said, let the dead bury the dead. For indeed we are born in death. And for this reason is it required for us to be born again before it is possible to enter into the Kingdom of God (Life). As Jesus said, A man must be born of water and spirit before he can enter into the Kingdom of God.. This is to say, he must be born of flesh and then of spirit, which is consciousness. For this reason when a child is born in this kingdom, he knows not his name nor his father's, but must learn it. Even as we are beginning to learn our Heavenly Father. For all shall be revealed in due season. Even as Christ proclaimed, it is so. Let no man deceive you. Jesus said, even before the foundation of the earth, I am. This is because when God created all things, even Adam, He knew of the fall and created Christ for the salvation of man (Adam). For God desires to dwell with man forever and has promised to "Redeem" him and take him into eternity with Him. For Jesus said, My Father's House has many Mansions and I go to prepare a place for you, if I prepare a place for you, I will return to receive you unto Me, so that where I am, you may be also. If it were not so I would tell you. Let your heart rejoice, for this is the Lord's doing and none other. For there is no other way to life then this. Let me further explain, Many questioned as to how Adam could fall, being that he was made perfect, for God can not make a mistake. Indeed, God is "perfect". We are that which is imperfect. Yet we are made perfect in Faith. For Faith is counted as righteousness, and Faith is given through Grace. It is written that Faith is the substance of things hoped for, the evidence of things not seen. For this reason we do not understand God's Mystery of all things, least there would be no need of Faith, or Christ, the High Priest over the house of God. But that in due season would all things be revealed. For Adam was made perfect for God's purpose. As Jesus said, If a kernel of corn is put into the ground and dies, many come forth, but if not, it will remain "alone". For this reason God knew of Adam's fall. Consider this, God created Adam and told him, he may eat from any tree of the garden, but one. The tree of Good and Evil. Howbeit, that God would create a tree that has Good and Evil? This mystery shall truly unfold before you in due season. For the time is at hand and even now is moving quickly. To explain of Adam, he desired not to disobey God the Father and was not tempted of the tree of Good and Evil. Then in due season God made Adam to go into a deep sleep and removed a rib from him and made Woman. Now some say that it was woman who made Adam fall, but there is a greater Truth. If God removed a rib from Adam, then he was divided. This should explain, Jesus said a house divided <u>must fall</u>. After Adam was divided he was tempted of the tree of Good and Evil. And could not overcome. Now there are those who say that Adam would not be forgiven of his transgression against God. Jesus said, that all things spoken against the Father or the Son will be forgiven, but he who blaspheme against the Holy Spirit it will not be forgiven him. Not in this world nor the next. Consider this, Adam was given two sons. Cain then Abel. Adam raised his sons in the ways of righteousness, and they both gave offerings unto the Lord . Abel was accepted of the Lord, but Cain's time had not yet come. For the Lord God said unto Cain, if thou doest well, shall thou not be accepted? And if thou doest not well, sin lieth at the door. Consider also that Jesus said, Some of the first shall be last and the last shall be first. So Cain's countenance fell and in his wroth he slew Abel. Howbeit, that Abel was righteous, if he came forth from Adam. One who has fallen from God and is not perfect . For righteousness is of perfection and how can that which is imperfect bring forth perfection. That which is impossible for man is possible for God. Indeed, Abel was righteous. For Jesus said; all the blood shed upon the earth, from the blood of righteous Abel unto the blood of Zacharias shall be required of this last generation. For it is written that God blessed Adam and Eve and said, Be fruitful and multiply and replenish the earth and subdue it. Again I say, Adam indeed was created perfect for God's purpose. To this end is it so that God would forgive Adam's transgressions, for Christ came for the lost and sick and to raise up <u>every man</u> unto the Judgment and <u>every</u> <u>man's</u> works shall follow him. In this consider also God gave unto Adam a third son, for the first son became lost and dwells in the land of Nod. (meaning, land of wandering) and Adam raised Seth in the ways of righteousness. Will not Adam's works follow him in the Resurrection? For the Resurrection is the Resurrection of the dead (lost, fallen from God). All men, even Adam, the Father of all flesh. Indeed so, for Jesus said, not everyone that saith unto me, Lord, Lord, shall enter into the Kingdom of Heaven, <u>but he that doeth the will of My Father which is in Heaven</u>. Is it not the will of our Father in Heaven that we teach our children the ways of our Lord? And if you will consider with your heart, you will hear that Christ was even before Adam, least Adam would not have begotten sons. For when a child enters into this kingdom he knows not who he is, or where he is from, nor can he care for himself. For this reason God the Father puts His Love in our hearts and minds to care for them and teach them. Even as we have been taught. For they are young in body and spirit. For Jesus said, a spirit (consciousness) in this kingdom, knoweth not whether it is here or there. Now if we can find within our hearts the desire to teach our children, will not the Father the more so teach us likewise and did He not send Our Lord and Savior to suffer for our sins. For it is the Lord that made the few to see and the many to be blind.. Even so Lord, it is Thy Power which Redeems our <u>souls</u> unto Thy Goodness

Amen.......

As I take pin in hand I praise thy Holy Spirit. In the book of Revelation it is written that a reed like unto a rod was given unto John to measure the temple of God, and the altar, and them that worship therein. But the court which is without the temple leave out, and measure it not. For it is given unto the Gentiles. My fellow-servants, hear and understand. The reed like unto a rod is a measure of time given unto John, for which his fellow-servants and our Lord walked even the prophets. For they (the Jews) are the chosen people of God. This is to say, the temple of God. And the altar is the sufferings of that people, even the sufferings of Jesus, our Lord and Savior. For He was and is the gift upon the altar. Who came through the seed of the Jews. That God's word might be fulfilled, even so Father

Amen.......

Now the courtyard is given unto the Gentiles. For this reason there was no temple. For the Gentiles had not yet become a people of God. For they knew not yet the Lord Christ. This measure of time had not yet come. Consider this, Jesus said that the promise of power would be given unto the Gentiles. For a Mighty Nation would raise up, and within it the Laws of the Saints. For this spiritual City indeed is the Camp of the Saints. Let me explain. This nation was conceived of the Saints and perceived of our founding forefathers. For the foundation of our laws was heard by men, but given from Heaven. This nation has been built on one saying, In God we trust. Thank not our forefathers, but God the Father and His Christ. Amen... Now in the time of the (2) two witnesses, when they shall walk upon the land among the Gentiles for (3 1/2) three and one half years, in sackcloth (laymen, common) and their power given, they shall reveal the first Woe and the beginning of Woes. For they are <u>One</u> with the Truth and the Father. For He alone has prepared them. And then this Nation must fall. For this one who ascends out of the Bottomless Pit shall make war against them and shall overcome them and kill them. For the Gentiles are not the first, but the last to become the Sons of God. The first people were the Jews, for this reason in Heaven was a temple, but in the courtyard was none. Jesus said that there was another flock and that they would be added unto the flock to make one fold. Hear and understand. In Revelation it says that many peoples, and kindreds and tongues and nations would become God's people. That is to say Gentiles. And that like the chosen people, we would become a temple to God. To say chosen, is to say through those people you would see God's repeated Truth and know He is

Lord. The time has come and now is, that the Mystery of God is to be understood. For great complexity is upon the Nations and upon men's hearts. This One who walks among us will tell us of things that men will not want to hear. For He will take men's self-righteousness from him, and glorify God with it. Because this One of whom I speak is in Spirit and he who has an ear to hear shall hear Him as He speaks. Now in this same time comes another who will give the world a false hope that peace has come. Let me speak more plainly. The Lord God, goes from the first to the last and then back to the first. In this reasoning we all become equal one to another. For we all have a part of God within us. And to each will receive their time, should they show patience and faith of the Saints. For the time comes and even now moves quickly, that all shall bow and confess Christ Lord, for it shall be revealed to All, in due season. If it has been revealed to any man, let him also have patience for him that has not yet understanding and to be not puffed up nor boasting, but to put his faith and understanding to God's seasons for He will speak to All who are able to listen. And to them who can not hear, they too have a part in God's Mystery. Let them receive it. For each is worthy of his hire and shall fulfill it. For there is good and evil and each is allowed by God and is His Mystery to fulfill His purpose. Know this with certainty, that if you can find a love in your heart that persist and will not die, and in this love you can find compassion for those you know around you, be then assured that you are among those that seek the Truth, for love has many levels. But those who are fearful of love or hide compassion, because they think that they will be used and hurt, know not Truth nor trust God. Do not think that you must know the greatest Love of All, or else you will not know Love. For it is not so. Only God knows the Greatest Love. For it is He and He alone that knows Himself, but He shares it unto the Son and He likewise unto the Saints and they likewise unto us. Amen. For Love is like no other spirit. It yields unto others, yet persists even without end. Love can be hidden, but it can not be killed and it continually appears where you would not think it could be. It is not understood because it is of God, and who knows the consciousness of God? No man, not even the Angels of Heaven. Let this not trouble you, but rather lift your spirit, for the Lord desires to give you His Kingdom, His Mighty Love that you might have Life and have it more abundantly. Let not the times and seasons deceive you. For many things must come to pass and great tribulations, but you can find rest and peace within you. Look not into the world, for it is not there, even so Father

Amen and Amen.......

My fellowself, what I am trying to say is this. Because of this season of time, there is to be great distress. Clean first the inside, so that the outside might be clean also. This is only to say, there are many lies in the mind that you <u>must hear, but need not believe</u>. When one of your fellow-beings, says or does an offensive thing to you, think not that it is he, but a spirit of this time. Hold it not against him for he too is a fellow-servant and if it is not his time to know this and believe it, then he is being deceived by that dark spirit, and if you are offended then you are like him and must show like spirit, but if it is your time to know the true spirit, *then you can help comfort this one who is caught up in distress, and with the power of the Holy Spirit, cast out this darkness within your fellow-self. Know the Truth. That there is but "One" true spirit and "One" who is evil. How shall you fill your mind? Make the tree good or make the tree evil. How will you consider things? Shall you believe that there are many against you, or trust that God shall guard you against this one who desires to deceive you. For he appears to be many, of great number. And God appears to be of few numbers. Yet know the Truth. For God's <u>Mercy</u> is also in you. Have you not heard, that the Kingdom of God is within you? It is so. Be then as the wise man who built his house on the rock, so that when the Great Storm comes it will not be washed away. The house is your mind and the rock is the Truth you <u>must believe</u>. The house will hear the storm on the outside, but also the Truth you built it on. Know then who the offense is of that you might not become as he, but as Christ, who is within you.*

Amen...

Yet know the Truth. For God's "Forgiveness" is also in you. Have you not heard? The Kingdom of God is within you. It is so. Then forgive all men who offend you, and be as the wise man who built his house on the rock, so that when the Great Storm comes onto you, your house will not be swept away. My fellow-self, the rock is Christ, in you. Let your mind know this Truth. Let His house be your house. He knocks upon your door. Let Him in that He might sup with you and you with Him.. That is to say, eat of this Truth. It is His. Let it be yours also. "Believe" it, and it becomes so. <u>Live it</u>, and then you'll "believe" it. Therefore the house becomes one with the rock it is built on. When the Great Storm comes unto your house, it will stand and not move. You, the house, will hear the storm on the outside, but also the Truth (the rock) you "trust" it on. Know then who the offense is of, so that you might not become as he, but as Christ, who is within you. Even so Lord, it is your day of Glory and the world's day of Great Darkness. For this spirit of darkness is given his hour and he will indeed use it against us. Where then is our salvation? In the Lord God Almighty, and the rock you have given. Let us stand upon it, oh Lord, in thy Faith, and in thy Holy Spirit.

Amen....

Oh children of Light, hear my words and let them find place in you. For the time is before you that there is great darkness. Let not the light of your eye be of this spirit. Come out of her my children. Oh hear and understand with the heart of your Heavenly Father. Let your eye see not this evil spirits ways of anger, hatred, revenge and offenses. Show the light of your Heavenly Father. To be slow to anger, quick to forgive, to express compassion and mercy on those that are not able to understand the times and the seasons of the world. For the hearts of men are their minds, which is easily deceived by this Great Evil spirit. And the heart of God is in every man, because it is One Heart. Its ways can be of our minds, and therefore our hearts. Believe in the Lord Jesus, and be like-minded. For He gave to us the Saints by praying unto the Father that He would not take them out of the world, but leave them as a light unto the world, that we might understand and "believe" and endure this "season" which has come

14

upon us. Look unto the world and see the eye for which the world is looking out of. I am not asking anyone to trust a man, but rather a "true spirit". For man can only reflect the spirit he believes in. If men believe only in men, then he is "doomed". For the spirit of man is fallen from God, and he is full of darkness in himself. Put then the light of God in you, and know what to "believe". For the time is Now, for Great Offenses and no man in himself can defy it. Father against his son, Mother against her daughter, Mother-in-law against her daughter-in-law, nation against nation, kingdom against kingdom. For no man will be able to help another man. Only the Spirit of Truth, God's gift to man can help us. But we must "believe" and "trust" in God. To do this is to know this day <u>must</u> come. For God has proclaimed it to be. And it will come, no matter what we do to prevent it. Even if we all turn to God's Truth, it still must come. Where then is our salvation? It is in the Lord Jesus. Reflect His ways. Be not offended of your fellowman, for a dark spirit dwells in him. And it desires to deceive you. For not all men can receive this Truth. For this evil spirit has manifested himself as a nation and will raise up to destroy the earth. For this day is given him by God and he will have it. Even as God allowed him his day with Job. For is it not written that this old serpent, the devil was bound in the bottomless pit until a certain day, then turned loose for a short season? Know then the "season" . Look upon the world and know it has come unto you. Let not your heart be fearful, for the Lord God is still with you. Even until the end. Know then what to believe. For the time is that you must hear offenses, but believe them not of your fellowman. Judge not this day, but "witness" it only. The Lord has overcome it.

Amen and Amen.......

Lord God of Glory and Power and Wisdom, with honor and strength and blessings, giving riches and peace and love stored within Thy Spirit of Truth, and put before the foundation of Grace, for the sake of man. Thy hour of Revelation has come. Now is the time for All, who might hear and understand. For the <u>seven seals</u> are of <u>Christ</u>, and were <u>fulfilled</u> in the <u>times</u> of <u>Jesus</u>, our <u>Lord</u> and His disciples. For it was done of spirit and therefore not seen of men. As Jesus said unto Nathanel; verily, verily I say unto you, <u>hereafter</u> you shall <u>see heaven open</u> and the <u>angels</u> of God <u>ascending</u> and <u>descending</u> upon <u>Son</u> of <u>Man</u>. Indeed, our Lord proclaimed it, and it was so. It is written that John, the beloved disciple, while in the spirit was taken up and beheld in the midst of the throne and of the four beast, and in the midst of the elders, stood a lamb, "As it <u>had been slain</u>", this is to say the angel of Christ, not Jesus the man. Least it would have said, like Son of Man. And this lamb having seven horns and seven eyes, which are the seven spirits of God sent forth into all the earth. For this one "only" had the power to loosen the seven seals of this Book. This book being the Book of Time, which is the <u>Mystery</u> of the <u>Creation</u> of <u>God</u> . The seven horns are the sufferings this one would bear, which is the curse of God, put unto Man for his transgressions. The seven eyes are the seven spirits of God, for whom this one shall have understanding and strength to proclaim it.

<u>First Seal</u>: *A white horse and one with a bow and a crown to go forth conquering and to conquer, Jesus as a young boy to go forth and do what no one has done before. To truly know the difference between Good and Evil. To gather God's Truth, which was scattered among men so that it might be hidden. To go forth conquering and to conquer. To do His Father's Business.*

<u>Second Seal</u>: *A red horse and one who takes peace from the earth by reason of Power, for a Great Sword was given Him. Jesus as a man, who came not to give peace unto the earth, but rather division. For peace of the earth was a cloak of sin. As Jesus said; If I had not come and spoken to them, they had not had sin, but now they have no <u>cloak</u> for their <u>sin</u>. If I had not done among them the works which none other man did, they had not had sin, but now they have both seen and hated, both Me and My Father. For the Great Sword is the Truth and works of God. For men kill one another by taking this Truth, which Christ gave together and they seek to part it and make it non-effect. Desiring to change it and make it a different doctrine and a different gospel . Thereby dividing the house of God by traditions.*

<u>Third Seal</u>: *A black horse and one who has a pair of balances or scales in his hand. And a measure of wheat and three measures of barley, of each the cost made equal. Also the oil and the wine be not harmed or lessened by reason of the balances thereof. For as Jesus said; He was the Light of the world, but that He must return unto His Father. For us to walk in the Light while it was on the earth, that we might become children of Light. And as He returned unto the Father, the Prince of Darkness would come into the world. For as Jesus said; Now is the Judgment of this world. For now shall the Prince of this world be cast out of Heaven unto the earth. This darkness would be counter balanced by the Comforter or Holy Spirit, which would come by reason of the Son. For this reason did Jesus say; Nevertheless, I tell you the Truth; It is expedient for you (the Apostle's, and they who receive the Truth) that I go away, for if I go not away, the Comforter will not come unto you; but if I depart I will send Him unto you. This counter balance (Comforter, Holy Spirit) has and will correct that which the evil one seeks to do. To deceive the very elect. If it were possible. For it is not given for All to understand, yet "Faith" is given to All who seek to "believe". For Faith comes not from understanding, but understanding from Faith. This is the greater works. Now this Comforter is of the Father, sent by reason of the Son, who speaks not of Himself, but of the Spirit of Truth. Which proceeds forth from the Father. And this which I speak is the three measures of barley. The Bread (Life) of God. The wheat is but one measure, which is the spirit of the world and the bread thereof which is also the prince*

of this world, who shall indeed deceive his own. And seek also to hurt the wine and the oil. For the oil is the elect, that is to say the anointed, those with some understanding. And the wine is the fruit of the vine. That which shall be poured out unto the children in the last days. Even which is poured out within these words. For it is True Spirit. Even so Father.

Amen.......

Is it not so, that at night when you bring a light into your room that it will fill the room, but when you put it out, the room becomes immediately full of darkness? Light being one force and Darkness the other, and yet if you, balance one against the other you have Twilight, which is some understanding.

<u>Forth Seal</u>: *A pale horse and one whose name was Death, and Hell was with him. And they were given Power over the forth part of the earth, to kill with the sword, hunger, death and the beasts of the earth. And what shall I tell you of this seal. And what is the earth that it is in part. There is one part land, and there is one part sea, and yet another air, and the forth part is spirit. For the earth is a living thing. As Jesus said; A man sows seed into the ground, earth, and waits and the earth brings forth the harvest, for the earth has life within it. Therefore this evil one shall have power over the forth part of the earth and shall kill with sword, by deception of the Truth, which was given by Christ the Lord. By hunger, because there are those who so hunger for the Truth (Life) that they receive the half truth believing it has the whole and become faint by it, by reason of tribulation and offense. And by death, because they believe they are alive, not knowing they are indeed dead and seek to save that which they think is life, but is not. And therefore are savoring death. For what shall a man gain if he should own the whole world and lose his own soul. And the beasts of the earth, there are those that know the power of the spirit and use it for their own cruel and selfish reasons, even as a sorcerer. But these are of the high ones, even of old. Nevertheless, take these things and apply them unto the parable of the sower. And begin to understand. He that is of the wayside hears of the word and understanding it not, which is to say, will not consider it and enter into his heart, for Faith, which begets Patience. For to understand is to know and believe God is, was, and will be. Therefore by not understanding the word, the wicked one takes that which was sown in their hearts away. Now him of stony places. He receives the word with joy, but after a time because we have no root within ourselves "alone" we become offended. Not knowing that the word (Truth) when it is received, what also must come is tribulation and persecution. For the very sake of the word needs it be so. And through faith and patience does a great weight become a lesser one. As for he who is among*

17

thorns, the same is he that receives the word, but because he knows not that he is dead, but thinks he is alive and therefore needs to seek the riches of the world and must store these things for his well being and shares them not. He becomes deceived and the word is choked in him and he departs from the heart in the midst of him. To this man would I say; Give alms to such things as you have, and behold, All things are made clean unto you. And of course he of the good ground. He has found the Truth and understanding in his heart in the midst of him. For it is Holy Ground.. He will not hold on to Any Offense, though he will yet taste it. For the heart which is in the midst of him, the same is that new birth of your spirit (consciousness) which makes you a new creature. For this reason he of good ground will be fruitful. Some an hundred fold, some sixty-fold and some thirty-fold. Let not this taste of offense trouble your heart. But rather Praise God for the tribulation and it will leave you, quickly, even as darkness leaves the presence of the light.

Fifth Seal: *And under the altar was seen the souls of them slain for the word of God and their testimony. These are the same that were of old times, even the prophets. And among them the Saints, each that overcame the beast and the image of the beast, also the false prophet. For the Lord God promised each who would overcome, would rest of their labors. For it seemed that they received not their reward. Even Abraham, yet Jesus said he not only saw it, but was glad. For they are the first-fruits of God. Now of this seal did their souls, "true spirit", cry. How long oh Lord, and they were given white robes and to rest yet a little season. For they were of the Former and the Latter is yet to come. This is to say, let the sowers and the reapers, rejoice together as one. And the white robes given them, was and is God's Righteousness, and they are glad and are able to rest because of it.*

Sixth Seal: *A great earth quake; and the sun became black as sackcloth, and the moon became as blood; The earthquake is Mount Zion being shaken. To say those on High. And the sun is a star darkened or angel that no longer gives forth light. To say the shining one. And the moon is a servant of the sun and reflects its power. Likewise, this Evil One, before hand had power in heaven and it was taken from him and his power is now only of earth, even of men. Now men's power is in their blood, therefore it has become Satan's power and the moon as blood reflects its master's power. To say he of low degree. The seals had begun while Jesus was yet among us, and as His Angel in Heaven broke the Seals, Jesus the man became aware of the Truth, and His Power of Light became greater and His Works likewise. He was and is the Angel ascending from the east. The seven (7) Seals are the wrath of God as promised to the prophets, but*

18

not to destroy man, but the Evil one. So God had an Angel ascending from the east saying with a loud voice to the four angels, to whom it was given to hurt the earth and sea to delay (stop). For this was the First Death and Resurrection. For which many things happened, but only in spirit and therefore not seen of men. For this reason the Seventh Seal came with silence for a space of an half hour. The many stars that fell to earth, was Satan and his angles. Also the Mystery of the Fig tree casting her untimely fruit. For Satan's fruit is indeed untimely. What God has said, He would do to men (those who sin), He did to Satan and his angels, (The Sixth Seal). Now the Vials are the Wrath of God made manifest. Revelation 15:4. This is to say, after Satan was cast out of Heaven, onto the earth. For while he was in heaven, he stood before the throne of God, continually to accuse and find fault before God Himself. Yet being cast onto the earth, he could not find God, even though God is here, just hidden so no one can see Him. For as Jesus gave us a parable, The Father is always with us, even until the end. For the Holy Spirit, even the Spirit of Truth is the Comforter, even as the Spirit of Truth is the Father, as Christ proclaimed, it is so. For God's wrath is not to the world, for He loved the world and gave His only begotten Son to save it. His wrath is to this One He has cast onto the earth. So His wrath was not manifested until after the Accuser was cast onto the world. Therefore the Vials were to the First Death (Resurrection), which could not come to completion until all the Saints had died. Which is John the beloved disciple. For the First Death, as it is written, the beast and the false prophet were cast into the Lake of Fire and the dragon (Satan) was cast into the bottomless pit. Yet in Revelation 16:13, it is written: I saw three unclean spirits like frogs come out of the mouth of the dragon, the beast and the false prophet. Therefore the Vials were of the First Death (Resurrection) made manifest and the Seals that which cast Satan and his Angels into the earth. And the trumpets are indeed of the Last Days. Even during the thousand years, which many think is yet to come.

*** To explain again the events that brought all these things into being, I should put them like this: The first Seal was Jesus as a young boy going about His Father's business as it is written in Luke 2:49. This including the missing (18) eighteen years of Christ. To this cause was He described as one on a white horse and a bow in his hand. For he freed his children not by power, nor by might but by His Spirit. For He was given a Crown and this Crown was and is His Authority. And with it He went forth conquering and to conquer. Now the second Seal was Christ during His Ministry of three and one half years (3 1/2). For He said that He came not to give peace, but to bring division. As it is written in Luke 12:51. And because of this, men would kill one another. Father against son and mother against her daughter. Yes a house divided, three against two and two against three. And the Great*

Sword given Him is the Word of God fulfilled, which is His Truth accomplished in Him and by Him. As to the third Seal, this was the time spoken of where the Lord said it was <u>expedient</u> for you that I go away. For if I go not away, the <u>Comforter</u> will not come unto you. This is written in John 16:7 thru 16:16. This Comforter (Holy Spirit) is He on the black horse with a pair of balances in His hand, which are the works done through the disciples (Church) <u>that the gates of hell shall not prevail against them</u>. For when Christ Jesus ascended unto Heaven He said wait in Jerusalem until Power from on High should come. This being the Holy Spirit. Act 1:8 But ye shall receive power, after that the Holy Ghost is come upon you: and ye shall be witnesses unto me both in Jerusalem, and in all Judaea, and in Samaria, and unto the <u>uttermost part of the earth</u>. Which came on the day of Pentecost. And the Lord also said to the disciples that He would not talk much to them because the prince of the world cometh, and hath nothing in Him. This meaning that the <u>Holy Spirit</u> would work <u>against</u> the working of the <u>prince</u> of the <u>world</u>, because he desires to destroy and replace the <u>Lord's Doctrine</u> with his <u>own</u>. This being the (1) one measure of <u>wheat</u> and the (3) three measures of <u>Barley</u> is the <u>Lord's doctrine</u>, which the Evil One would have you to believe that the cost is <u>equal</u>, but one is unto <u>Life</u> and the other is unto <u>Death</u>. And see thou <u>Hurt</u> not the <u>Oil</u> and the <u>Wine</u>. The <u>Oil</u> being the <u>Anointed</u> and the <u>Wine</u> being that which is poured out unto the <u>Children</u> in the <u>Last Days</u>. Now as to the fourth Seal and the meaning thereof: As it says, his name is <u>Death</u> and <u>Hell</u> followed with him. For Satan was wroth when the Lord of Glory received <u>His Thrown</u> and removed this One from the presence of the Thrown. For he could not anymore accuse the brethren before the Thrown of God. This caused him to go stand before the face of the Woman (Church, remnant of her seed). For the fourth part of the earth is "Spirit" and this Evil One would take the Word given (Sword) and try to change it and deceive many, as it was spoken of earlier. And to this cause, that is to say his deeds upon the earth concerning the Woman (remnant of her seed, Church) brought his own judgment onto himself by reason of the <u>Holy Spirit</u> and the <u>Works</u> therein. As these things continued, that is to say the balancing of works, then the fifth <u>Seal</u> was opened which gave rest to all those of <u>old</u> even the <u>prophets</u> and the <u>First Fruits</u>, which are spoken of in Rev. 12:4. And his tail drew the third part of the stars of heaven, and did cast them to the earth. This being from the First Estate. The reasoning for this is because if <u>he</u> the <u>dragon</u> cast a <u>third part</u> of the <u>stars</u> of <u>heaven</u> to the earth. Then they were <u>not his angels</u>, but <u>rather</u> the <u>First Fruits</u> which was <u>given</u> to <u>Christ</u> <u>by</u> the <u>Father</u>, even as the Lord said, it is so. And I tell you a Truth, these are the same from Ancient of Days. Now in the Regeneration of Son of Man, the Lord came for the First Fruits of which is the Church (the woman with the Crown of Twelve Stars) For He was <u>caught up</u> unto <u>God</u> until the <u>passing</u> of <u>time</u> and <u>witnessed</u> "Our Beginning" and to this cause is it written: Let <u>us</u> make <u>man</u> in <u>Our Image</u> and <u>Likeness</u>. And also this in Rev. 3: 14 And unto the angel of the church of the Laodiceans write; These things saith the <u>Amen</u> the <u>faithful</u> and <u>true witness</u>, the beginning of the <u>Creation</u> of <u>God</u>; Now in the time appointed the Seals were broken (Opened) by the Lion of the tribe of Juda, the root of David. A Lamb as it <u>had been slain</u>. Having <u>seven horns</u> and <u>seven eyes</u>, which are the <u>seven Spirits</u> of <u>God</u>

sent forth into all the earth. And along with this statement do I say that Rev. 12:1 thru 12:6 are the events which happened during the <u>First Estate</u> when <u>Lucifer</u> changed the <u>Light</u> thereof which brought all things to <u>Not</u>. And in the <u>Regeneration</u> of <u>all things</u> has it been made possible to be fulfilled. For <u>His Words</u> will not <u>return</u> to <u>Him</u> <u>empty</u> and <u>Void</u>, but <u>fulfilled</u>. Now the sixth Seal is that which casts Satan and his Angels into the earth, which is also mentioned in Rev. 12:7 thur 12:9.; 7 And there was war in heaven: Michael and his angels fought against the dragon; and the dragon fought and his angels, 8 And prevailed not; neither was their place found any more in heaven. 9 And the great dragon was cast out, that old serpent, called the Devil, and Satan, which deceiveth the whole world: he was cast out into the earth, and his angels were cast out with him. And again Rev. 6: 12-13 And I beheld when he had opened the sixth seal, and, lo, there was a great earthquake; and the sun became black as sackcloth of hair, and the moon became as blood; 13 And the <u>stars</u> of <u>heaven</u> <u>fell</u> unto the <u>earth</u>, even as a <u>fig tree casteth</u> her <u>untimely figs</u>, when she is <u>shaken</u> of a <u>mighty wind</u>. Now after Satan found himself casts into the earth. He and his Angels found the High Places upon the earth. And they persecuted the woman which brought forth the man child. Rev. 12:13. After this came the Seventh Seal, when there was silence in heaven about the space of half an hour. This was the coming of Christ to receive His own as He told the Twelve in Mat. 10: 23 But when they persecute you in this city, flee ye into another: for verily I say unto you, Ye shall <u>not have gone over the cities</u> of <u>Israel</u>, <u>till</u> the Son of man <u>be come</u>. This being the secret coming of Christ to receive the foundation of the Church, even the First Fruits for the marriage of the Lamb. After receiving the last of the Twelve, then came the pouring of the Vials, which closed heaven. Rev. 15: 8 And the temple was filled with smoke from the glory of God, and from his power; and <u>no man</u> was <u>able</u> to <u>enter</u> into the <u>temple</u>, <u>till</u> the <u>seven plagues</u> of the <u>seven</u> <u>angels</u> were <u>fulfilled</u>. Now while heaven was closed to the earth and the inhabitants thereof, the marriage of the Lamb took place. As the Lord gave us a parable concerning the marriage. That it would take place in secrecy, because in the parable the Lord said that none of those who were not worthy would have any part of the marriage. Which was during this time the Vials were poured out. And the Sixth Vial tells us at what time this is being done. As it is written in Rev. 16: 13 And I saw three unclean spirits like frogs come out of the mouth of the dragon, and out of the mouth of the beast, and out of the mouth of the false prophet. This showing that the Vials are indeed of the First Death (Resurrection) because this took place before the twelve thrown judgment which is the First Resurrection. Now after the Vials were completed, heaven was opened. As it is written in Rev. 19: 11 And I saw heaven opened, and behold a white horse; and he that sat upon him was called <u>Faithful</u> and <u>True</u>, and in righteousness he doth <u>judge</u> and make <u>war</u>. And again in Rev. 19: 15 And out of his mouth goeth a sharp sword, that with it he should smite the nations: and he shall rule them with a rod of iron: and he treadeth the winepress of the fierceness and wrath of Almighty God. And in Rev. 19:19-20. 19 And I saw the beast, and the kings of the earth, and their armies, gathered together to make war against him that sat on the horse, and against his army. 20 And the beast was taken, and with him the false prophet that wrought miracles before him, with which he deceived them that had received the mark of the beast, and them that worshipped his image. These both were cast alive into a lake of fire burning with brimstone. This showing that the war was on earth not heaven. And that heaven was closed and then opened, which is only to say: Was done in Spirit and therefore not seen of men. And then, of course the dragon (Satan) was casts into the _Bottomless Pit_. Rev. 20:2. Now in Rev. 20:4-5 it is written: 4 And I saw _thrones_, and they sat upon them, and _judgment_ was given unto them: and I saw the souls of them that were beheaded for the witness of Jesus, and for the word of God, and which had not worshipped the beast, neither his image, neither had received his mark upon their foreheads, or in their hands; and they lived and reigned with Christ a thousand years. 5 But the rest of the dead lived not again until the thousand years _were finished_. This is the _First Resurrection_. This saying that those spoken of in Rev. 20:4 _lived again_ with Christ a thousand years. And after the Millennium those which _were dead_ would live again in the (_Second Death Resurrection_) along with the remnant upon the earth. That is to say, the (60) sixty fold and the (30) thirty fold. For they are of the Second Resurrection (Death) and the time of the (2) Two Witnesses. Now near the end of the First Resurrection, Trumpets (1) one thru (4) four are sounded in Spirit and therefore not seen of men. For it is the fifth Trumpet that begins the Second Death (Resurrection). All of this to show that the Millennium is not of peace, but Judgment. And that the Trumpets are of both the First and Second (Death) Resurrection. **

Amen.......

Oh Praise Thee Lord of Harvest for thy witness of Truth has come. For thou Art the Holy Spirit, even the Spirit of Truth. And here is the Wisdom of He who is First and also Last. The Vials began after the last of the foundation of the church was received (Translated) into the Kingdom of God. For this cause did Jesus say unto the (12) twelve in Matthew 26:29 (in the day of the Last Supper); I tell you I will no more drink of the fruit of the vine, until I drink it with you "New" in My Father's Kingdom. This also being the Marriage of the Lamb unto the Church (Wife, foundation). And to this cause was the wine "New". For the vials are two (2) fold in purpose. First it is the Wrath of God made manifest unto this Evil One and his angels and also his remnant (flesh). Meaning that it is first accomplished of spirit and then of flesh. And secondly its purpose is to prevent any of the inhabitants of the earth to partake of the Marriage. Even the dragon and his angels who are cast "into" the earth. For the seat (throne) of Satan is the mind of man, and where man is so also is his Master. Yet there is One who is over him. And He is Lord of Lords and King of Kings, even so Glorious One

Amen and Amen......

So that those of you who are weak in Faith might become strong these things are being revealed unto you. For in Revelation 15:8 it is written; and the temple was filled with smoke from the Glory of God, and from His Power, And "no" man was able to enter into the temple, till the seven plagues of the seven Angels were fulfilled. This meaning that Heaven was "closed" unto the inhabitants of the earth, All inhabitants. Therefore the vials (closed) sealed Heaven and the Marriage took place. And was witnessed by the inhabitants of Heaven "Only". Now after the vials were fulfilled, Heaven was opened. As it is written in Revelation 19:11 ; And I saw heaven opened, and beheld a white horse; and he that sat on him was called Faithful and True. And in Righteousness he doth judge and make war. This being the First Judgment and/or Resurrection by which such Battle took place after the vials. Not before, because the beast, false prophet and the dragon have three (3) unclean Spirits come out of their mouth in the sixth (6) vial. Which is before the beast and false prophet are cast "Alive" into the Lake of Fire. And Satan is bound and sealed in the bottomless pit. And as for those who shall reign on the earth, as it is written in Revelation 5: 9 -10; And they sung a New Song, saying, thou art worthy to take the book, and to open the seals thereof; for thou wast slain, and has redeemed us to God by thy blood out of every Kindred, and Tongue, and people, and Nation; And has made us unto Our God, Kings and Priests: And we shall reign on the earth. For I tell you a Truth, these are before the Throne of God and their remnant do reign upon the earth and their Light doth Shine. Do you not yet understand? For these have been Redeemed and God would not cast them unto the earth, but through them shall their Remnant reign upon the earth. Oh Thank Thee Father of Creation for thou "Only" Art Holy and thy ways are wonderous and thy Righteousness is Most High. For thou Art the Redeemer and the Holy One and the King of Saints. For you have taken Your Great Power and do Reign forever and ever, even so Father.

Amen.......

And as to the remnant upon the earth, consider Revelation 12 and its meaning of the Woman and the remnant of her seed. For the Woman clothed with the Sun and the Moon under her feet, and upon her head a crown of twelve (12) stars: Is the Church of Our Lord Christ and the crown of twelve (12) stars are the Apostles, and the Raiment of the Sun is the Light God has sent unto the earth for Salvation, and the Moon is under her feet, because she is raised up above the earthly and shall shine forth her Light unto the earth in the night (evening) of the Lord's Great day. For the Lord's day has a morning and an evening, even as it was in the beginning. To this Truth there are two (2) Resurrections and also that Christ Jesus is of the Morning and the Bright and Morning Star of the Lord's Great day. Which is of the First Resurrection. And the woman being with child cried, travailing in birth, and pained to be delivered. And this manifesting to be, also brought forth the Evil One (A Great Red Dragon) whose Power was able to draw a third of Heaven into his Will. For he desired to devour the woman's child as soon as it was born. And the dragon stood before the Woman which was ready to be delivered. And she brought forth a man child (which is Christ Jesus): and her child was caught up unto God, and to His Throne. This meaning that Satan (the dragon) deceived men that they would kill this man child (Christ Jesus) and to persuade them to destroy the church. For Satan knew not that God the Father would raise up this <u>man</u> <u>child</u> Christ Jesus in the regeneration. For had he known he would not have shed His blood, because it is by this blood that Satan was cast out of Heaven. Indeed, Satan was in Heaven even until Christ Jesus was raised up unto God. Then there was war in Heaven, and Michael and his Angels fought against the dragon and his angels. And they (dragon and his angels) prevailed not, neither was there place found anymore in Heaven. For if you can receive it, Michael and his Angels, the same are Jesus (the Lamb) and the First Fruits of God (144,000) one hundred and forty-four thousand that were redeemed from among men. Which came forth from the foundation of the earth (where Christ Jesus dwelled for three days and three nights). Now when the dragon saw that he was cast unto the earth, he persecuted the woman which brought forth the Man child (Christ Jesus). And to the woman were given two (2) wings of a great eagle, that she might fly into the wilderness, into her place, where she is nourished for a time, times, and half a time, from the face of the serpent. This meaning that the beast that rose up out of the sea which had one of his heads as it were wounded to death; and his deadly wound was healed. The same deceived men to persecute the church (woman that brought forth the Man child). And they tried to kill the church, but these men of a certain Nation (Romans) lost their Great Power and the church was given a time, and times and half a time to grow in her place, which is in the hearts and minds of all men who would receive her faith of Christ Jesus. Now the serpent cast out of his mouth water as a flood after the woman, that he might cause her to be carried away of the flood. And the earth helped the woman, and the earth opened her mouth, and swallowed up the flood which the dragon cast out of his mouth. And the meaning is this: the flood water which was cast out of the serpents mouth is a multitude of people or to say a Nation. For when the serpent saw he was cast onto the earth he persecuted the woman (church) and two (2) wings of a great eagle was given her that she (church) would be removed from the <u>face</u> of the _serpent_. This is only to say that the true church would be hidden from the face of the serpent after all of the Apostles were translated into Heaven. To say true church means Spirit (also concepts, beliefs). Because the Church was hidden from the serpent, he cast the flood waters from his mouth with the desire to carry the church (remnant of her seed) away as a people. Now this Nation (flood water) became a Mighty Nation even as Rome was a Mighty One and likewise would lose some of its power. This is not to say this Nation is an evil nation, just a deceived one. For as it is written All the Nations shall be deceived by this evil one. Yet there was a time when this evil one would not be able to deceive all the Nations. To this cause the church (woman) Lives and has grown strong. Nevertheless, if the serpent using this Nation or flood waters had succeeded, the world would have had a Great King and a Dead Church ruled by deception of this evil one. Now this Nation became Great,but the earth helped the woman (church, remnant) and swallowed up the flood waters, which is to say this Nation lost some of its power. This happened because the serpent went to prepare war with the remnant of her seed (church). This meaning many generations would pass, while the church (Spirit) grows and becomes strong. The Nation I speak of is Great Britain or the United Kingdom. Let not this truth become offensive to you. For Great Power and Authority was given to this evil one. Even so that he will deceive God's chosen people. As Jesus said: I come in My Fathers Name and you do not believe me. _Another_ will _come_ in _his own name_ and _him you will receive_. Consider this: Satan, the evil one desires his church and shall have it. To this cause did he bring forth the flood waters to convert the Lord's Church to his own. Yet he was not able because the church was married to the Lord in Heaven and as Jesus said, the gates of Hell will not prevail against it. It shall not see Death. So this evil one could not put his face before the church because the Lord is Greater then he. Because of the Truth this evil one went to prepare or set up the Abomination of Desolation for the remnant of her seed (church). For it is in the belief of this Evil One that he is able to change times and laws as it is written in Daniel 7:25 ; And that he shall wear out the Saints of the Most High and they shall be given into his hand until a time, and times and the dividing of times. For it was for this season that he prepared or set up the Abomination of desolation, that he might change times and laws. So that when the time of the twelve (12) throne judgment to fall did come that he might seal them even as he was sealed. This is only to say, that this Evil One desires to break the Laws and the Prophecy as it was given in the beginning. That he might make God the Father of Creation as himself. That is to say a "Liar". For he is this one who shall come in his own name and shall be received by many. He is even the one horn that had eyes, and a mouth that spake very great things. For it is given him to make war with the Saints of the Most High and to prevail against them. Yet it is not given him to destroy the Saints. Nevertheless, he believes that the power of the voice of the great words which he (the horn with eyes, and a mouth) spake would change times and laws. Yet, the Ancient of days shall sit and the Saints of the Most High shall possess the Kingdom forever even for ever and ever. What then is this Abomination of desolation and how shall we see it? As it is written in the Former days so also shall it be in the Latter days. Which is even now and has been for a time and times and the dividing of time. The Abomination of desolation is the Laws and beliefs of the Nations of the world. And the Laws and beliefs shall govern the people and they shall become an image of said Laws and belief. This is only to say that as in the time of Daniel (former days) so also shall it be in these times (latter days). This is to say the Night Vision of Daniel. There is three (3) Great Beasts (Nations) that come-forth upon the earth then shall come a fourth and he shall subdue the three (3) by reason of his greatness. For he comes from a far off and distant place. Now in him comes an Old One who has understanding of dark (Mysterious) sentences. The three (3) Beasts or Nations are the Major Powers of the world in this time and they have been influenced by the fourth power which has not made himself known yet, but shall very soon by reason of a great calamity that shall come upon the earth. It is written of in the table of stone in the land of Egypt. It is found on the Northeast side of the Kings Chamber. It shall bear witness of these sayings, yet there is a greater that shall bear witness of these sayings and of he who gives them unto you. Nevertheless, consider the beast that Daniel saw. The first was like a Lion and had eagles wings. After a passing of time the wings were plucked and it was lifted up from the earth and made to stand as a man and a mans heart was given it. This is to say that this nation shall raise up from another and part from it by reason of two (2) great wings of an eagle, which is only to say, God's promise of Liberty and Justice would be given unto this Great One (Nation). Yet the wings were plucked away in time only to be given unto the church (remnant of her seed). Nevertheless, this great one would be lifted up from the earth and made to stand as a man and a mans heart was given it. This meaning that this great nation would remain even until the end (lifted above the earth) and would seek to free All peoples, that is to say, to stand as a Man. For All peoples and kindreds and tongues, make up that which is Man. To say again, to let All men live in freedom. And to say a mans heart was given it, is only to say, this Great Nation shall desire and seek to lift mankind unto Lordship of the Kingdom, even as God had done in the beginning. This meaning that as a Nation of peoples and kindreds and tongues, they would seek to live together in peace not only for themselves, but also the world and all who live on it (mankind). Now the second beast was like unto a Bear and it raised up itself on one side and it had three ribs in the mouth of it between the teeth of it. And they said thus unto it. Arise and devour much flesh. This Great One (Nation) began with a coming together of three (3) peoples, which are the three (3) ribs in the mouth of the beast. Now these three (3) small ones had fear of being devoured and called a strong one to keep them as a Nation and to this cause was the beast (bear) raised up on one side. This also being the reason the three (3) ribs were in the mouth of it between the teeth of it. Because they desired to be a Great One and they the (3) three ribs said thus: Arise and devour much flesh. Which is to say this; because you are strong, become a Great One, make us become strong in you. So they were as a people led into One. The third beast, like a leopard, which had upon the back of it four (4) wings of a fowl; the beast had also four (4) heads; and dominion was given it. The third beast is the first of three to come upon the earth. And to that cause was dominion given unto it. This is only to say that their number upon the earth would be Most Great. They are of old and wisdom was given unto them. The four (4) heads are the four dynasties from which the wisdom came. And the four (4) wings of a fowl

26

are likewise four other dynasties which became their greatness That is to say their portion of the one thousand (1,000) years of Christ Reign in the midst of the First Resurrection. For it was in these four dynasties that this Great One (Nation) grew and its peoples became more one Kingdom rather than many, whose Traditions remain even to this day. Now the fourth beast or Great One is not raised up unto Greatness among men. To this cause is it more diverse than All the beasts before him. That is to say this beast being most unlike the three other beasts. The three other beasts were All from this world (Kingdom). And this was their likeness. Yet, the fourth beast is most unlike the rest. This Nation (Great One) is from old and to this cause his power is Great. Yea, it is by this Great One that the three beasts have their Kingdom taken away, but their lives remain for a time and season. As it is written in Daniel 7:12. As concerning the rest of the beasts, they had their dominion taken away: yet their lives were prolonged for a season and a time. This meaning that these three Nations would continue to live yet their power would be influenced by this fourth beast (Nation) that shall not reveal himself until after the <u>sixth trumpet</u> is sounded and a third of man should die. Then shall this Great One reveal himself and those who remain on the earth shall see and hear the Lying wonders of the God of the earth. For I tell you a Truth, he who has come is not Alone and his power is through an old one, even a Nation and he shall destroy wonderously. And he shall cast the Truth to the ground. Yea, He has come, but he is yet to reveal himself. Indeed, He has influenced the Nations upon the earth, even the peoples for whom God has given the promise of power and Authority and land of plenty which is the time of the Gentiles and the fruitfulness thereof. For the Nations I speak of are the three Major Powers of the earth today. That is to say, the United States of America is the first beast and the United Soviet Social Republic is the second beast and the third beast or Nation is the People's Republic of China. And the fourth beast comes to save the earth by reason of appearance and thereby transforming himself and being revealed as the God of the earth. Now consider in Revelation of the fifth trumpet and that an Angel come down from Heaven and has the Key of the Bottomless Pit and he has opened it. This being the end of the First Resurrection and the thousand years of sleep unto this Old One. For the seal that God has used upon this Old One was a deep sleep and to this cause he was not able to deceive the nations until he was awakened and I tell you now in Truth, when he was awakened so also was the seal of silence finished. For it was in that time that worldly knowledge began to increase and his Abomination of Desolation started to increase likewise. For it is worldly knowledge which this evil one uses to deceive All Nations. Yea, it is this knowledge for which this evil one trust in and He desires for you to trust in it also. Believe him Not! Do you not yet understand? Flesh and blood can not inherit the Kingdom of God, therefore seek not to save your body, but rather your <u>spirit</u> and in doing so you shall also be found with Life Eternal. To save your spirit is to trust in Christ the Lord, even as He trusted in the Father to give Him Faith and not worldly knowledge. To commend (Trust) His spirit unto His hands. Yea, it was worldly knowledge that Satan offered Jesus in the desert and Our Lord rebuked it and trusted in the Faith of God. For it is this Faith that brings strength of spirit. For it was this same Faith that Jesus spoke of while on the Cross, when He said: Father into thy hands I commend My Spirit. And consider also what was said by the chief priests: He trusted in God; let Him deliver him now, If He will have him: for he said, I Am the Son of God. Indeed, He trusted in God and God delivered Him and raised Him up, even as He shall raise us up in these the Last Days. Therefore, strengthen your spirit by reason of Faith of Christ Jesus and learn of His Ways and be like-minded. Let not the worldly knowledge deceive you, be ye wise in Christ Jesus and foolish in the knowledge of the world. Least your bands be made strong, which is the strength of the spirit. Learn not the precepts of men, but rather the indwelling Holy Spirit. For it is He who teaches the Faith of Our Lord Jesus Christ and He who strengthens Our Spirit that we might have Life in Him who is Alive. That we might have ears to hear and a heart to understand the Spirit of Truth. For behold the time and season has come unto us that the terrible one is brought to naught, and the scorner is consumed, and All that watch for iniquity are cut off: That make a man an offender for a word, and lay a snare for him that reproveth in the gate, and turn aside the just for a thing of naught. But first he must have his day, which is before us, then shall this time be, even so it is at the door. Yea, this fourth beast is the terrible one and when he is revealed the third Woe comes quickly. Nevertheless, this fourth beast has consumed the other three beasts by reason of influence for they have become the sorcerers, even as it is written in Revelation 6:8. And power was given unto them over the fourth part of the earth, to kill with sword, and with hunger, and with death, and with the <u>beasts of the earth</u>. For the three beasts of the earth have become one beast which is the fourth beast. And the three beasts have become sorcerers because they appear to have power and authority each to themselves, yet they are governed and controlled by the fourth beast who is yet to reveal Himself. And in the revealing He shall be transformed into an Angel of Light. Then you shall hear the voice of His words and the works of His Sorceries. And many of those who remain shall worship a Strange God and rejoice in a false peace and shall kill the only salvation left unto them. For the two (2) witnesses give testimony of this one who must come before He is revealed by God's hand. Yet, who was able to hear? And when His brightness is before them, who will understand that God has chosen this One for everlasting punishment. For He is the portion that bears the seed of Cain, who has gone out of the presence of God into the land of Nod. And to this one who became a builder of a Great City. Who named this Great Nation with a name that became Great in Heaven and before God. Even Enoch, the seventh son of Adam, who is Not, because God took him. Now to consider the Land of Nod, you must first consider the Creation for in it is the Mystery understood. If you look into the heavens (Universe) you find many galaxies, each being a heaven unto itself. They being the many heavens of Heaven. To this cause did Jesus speak of coming from one end of Heaven unto the other. This also applying to the Regeneration of Son of Man, even the replenishing of the Earth. For this One who is Revealed the same is he of old times. To this cause the Ancient One is with him. He who ascends out of the bottomless pit. And to this one and they who are in him do I say; And he who Rises out of the midst of the pit shall be caught in the snare. For the end must come, for the word came down from God (Creator) and He has spoken it. Will it not be so? Yet, there is One who said it was not so. For He could not endure *the words nor bear the Truth of it. To this cause did He Command that the words be not spoken. And that He should change the Laws and times concerning this so that His Commandment Might be Wisdom as it was on High. To this cause shall He have His day and hour as it was granted Him in the Day when He was created and became the Shining One. He stood before God (Creator) and Reflected the Light of Wisdom and Beauty, even unto the end of the Earth. Yet, in the passing of time came a New Song to be sung in Heaven for which only the First-fruits could learn and the Remnant thereof. To this cause did the seal of silence come that this Shining One could not stand before the Church nor learn the Song of Secrecy. Now as to and concerning the seventh seal and its half hour of silence: This is for the closing of Heaven which is to say the silent coming of Christ to receive the Church and the Marriage Supper of the Lamb(This is to say the Church being removed from the face of the serpent). For Jesus said unto the disciples: Verily I say unto you, Ye shall not have gone over the cities of Israel, till the Son of Man be come. And also this: ye have not chosen Me, but I have chosen you (disciples), and Ordained you, that ye shall go and bringforth fruit, and that your fruit should Remain:The first saying that He Jesus shall return after the disciples gather together those called unto the Marriage Supper of the Lamb. For Jesus said unto the disciples: I go to prepare a place for you, so that Where I am You may be Also. Then Jesus prayed unto the Father saying: Father, I will that they Also, whom thou hast given Me, be with Me where I am; that they may behold My Glory which thou hast given Me. And secondly the fruitfulness of the Church walking among men while they were gathering unto the Great Supper and that this fruit would remain and become the Remnant of her seed (Church). And it was this Remnant which was hidden from the face of the Serpent. And he went to prepare war with them. For they were yet to come, even the Last Generation. So Jesus came in silence to receive the Church (the disciples) and they that received them, and the fruit (Remnant) of them, Remained and became the Remnant of her seed (Church). For it was this same time that the Angel Ascending from the East, which sealed the one hundred and forty-four thousand (144,000) with the seal of the Living God, closed heaven by reason of the vials after receiving the Church. And they that remain "the remnant of her seed"; they were given two (2) wings of a Great Eagle to fly into the wilderness (times and seasons) to a place prepared of God. That the Serpent could not put his face before the Church, so he (Satan) went to prepare war with "the remnant of her seed". Because of the seventh seal of silence (secrecy) this Evil One (Satan) could not stand before "the remnant of her seed", even with the flood waters he could not prevail against them. Nevertheless, because of his works the vials were poured unto him and his kingdom. Know also, because he and his angels are spirit, this Wrath of God even as the seals, were done in spirit and therefore not seen of men. To this cause the world could not see the pouring of the vials unto the earth nor unto the men with the mark of the beast. And likewise the trumpets have been sounded in spirit even until the sounding of the fifth trumpet which is the first Woe and the beginning of the end of the seal of silence and the time for the father to come that he might be subdued unto and put under the Son (Christ) that the scripture might be fulfilled. Then cometh the end when He shall have delivered up the Kingdom of God, even the Father;*

when He shall have put down All Rule and All Authority and All Power. Let me explain in this manner; Jesus said as He prayed unto the Father; <u>Father</u>, thy hour is come; <u>glorify thy Son, that thy Son Also may glorify thee</u>: Then again He said unto the disciples: <u>all things</u> that the <u>Father hath</u> are <u>mine</u>: Therefore said I, that He (Spirit of Truth) <u>shall take of mine</u> and <u>shall shew it unto you</u>. Now if <u>All things</u> were given unto the Son then He has become the Father, even as He said unto Philip: Have I been so long time with you, and yet hast thou not known Me, Philip, he that hath seen Me hath seen the Father. For if the Father (who is Greater than the Son) gave <u>All things</u> unto the Son, even the Throne of All rule and All authority and All power, then indeed <u>All things</u> are subdued unto Him and indeed He hast delivered up the Kingdom to God, even the Father. For the Son of Man has received the Father and therefore became Him and the Father gave All things unto the Son and therefore became Him. To this cause did Jesus say unto the disciples concerning who shall sit to the right and to the left of Him: Ye shall indeed drink of My cup, and be baptized with the baptism that I am baptized with: but to sit on My Right hand and on My Left, <u>is not mine to give</u>, but it shall be given to them for whom it is <u>prepared of My Father</u>. For He has indeed been with us, even until the End. That the Scripture might be fulfilled: Jehovah, God Himself, shall come. Do you not yet know the Love of the Father unto the children? God the Father (Holy Spirit, He who sat upon the throne). Sent the Son while the wicked (Evil) were yet on High where He was. Then after this Evil One was cast unto the Earth and the Son was caught up unto the throne, on High. Then the Father(Holy Spirit) came unto the earth, even as the Evil One was cast down. For it is the Father Only, who is Greater than All. For is it not written that this Evil One prevails against the Saints, even the Holy people, for a time and times and the dividing of time. Yet, there is Christ who is Greater than this Evil One. By the Power and the Glory of God the Father of Creation who has put His Power and Glory into the Father of Godhead for whom the Son Has Glorified through the Name of the Holy Spirit, even the Spirit of Truth, being the third part of the Godhead, which is God the Father of Creation. So the Father (Holy Spirit) came, even as the Son was caught up unto the throne and remained that in the Last Days, He the Father of All flesh (Spirit of Adam) would manifest and then be received by the Son who sits upon the throne of the Father. That all might be fulfilled, for All must be delivered up, even the Father (Adam's Spirit). Indeed the Father must be in Him (Christ Jesus), even as it is written <u>I am in the Father</u> and <u>the Father in Me</u>. For I and my father are one. Indeed <u>all</u> things are subdued unto Him (Christ Jesus). For He is King of Kings and Lord of Lords. For the Holy One of Israel and the Only Redeemer is the Father and the Son. And the Holy Spirit is the Spirit of Truth which proceedith forth from the Father who is also one with the Son and it is <u>They</u> that have fulfilled All Works and All things are brought unto remembrance by reason of the Holy Spirit, even the Spirit of Truth, who speaks not of His own, but that which He hears, which is the Father, even the Son for <u>They</u> are One by the Power and Glory of He the Father of Creation and there is None who stand beside Him. For He is the potter and His Works do Honour Him, And it is He who has Framed with Understanding the heavens, even the Heaven of heavens. And it is He who gives Knowledge and teaches doctrine. As it is written in Isaiah

28:9 : Who shall he teach knowledge? And whom shall he <u>make</u> to understand doctrine? Them that are weaned from the milk, and drawn from the breasts. For precept must be upon precept, precept upon precept; line upon line, line upon line; here a little, and there a little: For with stammering lips and another tongue will He speak to this people. To whom He said, this is the <u>Rest</u> wherewith ye may cause the <u>weary</u> to <u>Rest</u>: and this is the refreshing: Yet they would not hear. Now it was not in the former days of Christ that these words were spoken with stammering lips and another tongue, but rather the latter days, even now by reason of one who is yet presently with you. For it was in the former days of Christ (First Resurrection) that Christ said unto the people; <u>This is the Rest</u> wherewith ye may cause the <u>weary to</u> <u>Rest</u>; and this is the <u>Refreshing</u>: yet they (unbelievers) would not hear. For the Rest and the Refreshing is Christ the Lord. As Jesus said unto the multitudes; come unto Me, All ye that <u>Labor and are heavy Laden</u>, and <u>I will give you Rest</u>. Take My yoke upon you, and learn of Me; For I am meek and lowly in Heart: And you shall find <u>Rest unto your souls</u>. For My yoke is easy, and My burden is Light. Indeed, He the Lord Christ spoke it unto All, even the unbelievers of the First Resurrection, which are Raised up again in the Last days (Second Resurrection), And in this day has He spoken it again with <u>Another</u> <u>tongue</u> <u>and</u> <u>Stammering</u> <u>Lips</u>. Yet they (unbelievers) will not hear. For the Word of the Lord is unto <u>them</u> precept upon precept, precept upon precept; line upon line, line upon line; here a little, and there a little: that <u>they</u> might go, and <u>fall backward</u>, and be <u>broken</u>, and <u>snared</u>, and <u>taken</u>. For in the Latter days as He speaks again unto <u>this people</u>, even <u>they</u> who should <u>live again after</u> the <u>thousand years</u> of <u>sleep</u>. For Just are the ways of the Lord. As it is written: For the Lord shall rise up as in Mount Perazim, He shall be wroth as in the Valley of Gibeon, that He may do <u>His works</u>, <u>His Strange Work</u>; and bring to pass <u>His Act, His Strange Act</u>. Now therefore be ye not Mockers, Least your bands be made strong: for I have heard from the Lord God of Host a consumption, even determined upon the whole earth. For <u>that time</u> and <u>that work</u> of the <u>Lord has come</u> for which few will understand yet many will enter in by reason of Faith. For the time is come that many must take on the appearance of death, Yea they must taste death, yet shall they live, even as Christ Lives. To this cause do I tell you the Earth shall become a fire and only a portion shall Remain. Then shall this One Reveal himself. Who shall cast the Truth onto the ground and who shall sit in the temple of God showing himself that He is God. Then shall the End come and the Everlasting take on form. Yea it shall be sudden, even in a moment. For the Recreation is from the Brightness of His Coming. To this cause is it written: And then shall the Wicked be Revealed whom the Lord shall consume with the Spirit of His Mouth, and shall destroy with the brightness of His coming. Even Him, whose coming is After the working of Satan with All power and signs and Lying wonders. Therefore Know also and understand that which is written in Isaiah 29:11 : And the <u>Vision</u> of <u>All</u> is become unto you as the words of a <u>book</u> that is <u>sealed</u>, which men deliver to <u>one</u> that is <u>learned</u> saying, Read this, I pray thee: And he saith, I <u>can not</u>; for it is <u>sealed</u>: And the <u>book</u> is delivered to him that is <u>not learned</u>, Saying, Read this, I pray thee: And he saith, <u>I am not learned</u>. For I tell you a Truth, the <u>sealed book</u> is that which we this day call the <u>book of Revelation</u>. And he to whom it was delivered, the same is *he that had some understanding and therefore Knew the book was sealed for a time, times and the dividing of times. Meaning of the First Resurrection. Now he who was not learned, the same is he of the Latter days (Last Days). For the things Revealed in the coming of the First Resurrection were again hidden by the Evil One who was cast out of Heaven as Christ was taken up. To this cause those of the Second Resurrection were not learned as the book was delivered unto them. Yet the time and season came unto this people and God has poured out His Spirit unto them and the blind are made to see through darkness and the deaf are made to understand. But, let not this <u>sealed book</u> trouble you for the Lord also said: Therefore, behold, I will proceed to do a <u>Marvelous Work</u> among this people, even a <u>Marvelous Work</u> and a <u>Wonder</u>: for the <u>Wisdom</u> of their <u>Wise men</u> shall <u>perish</u>, and the <u>understanding</u> of their <u>Prudent men</u> shall be <u>hid</u>. This meaning that the Knowledge of Men shall become foolishness and be cast off and the Knowledge which comes shall be concealed unto the few who seek to Rule. Yet sing in your Spirit for the time of the end is come. Yet a little to Witness and All shall be done. Consider Isaiah 29:15 : Woe unto them that seek deep, to hide their council from the Lord, And their works are in the dark, and they say, who seeth us? And who Knowth us? Surely your turning of things upside down shall be esteemed as the potter' s clay: for shall the work say of him that made it, He made me not? Or shall the thing framed say of him that framed it, He had no understanding? Now for those who can not discern the times and seasons God has given the World a sign as to when this day is upon you. Again Isaiah 29:17 : Is it not yet a little while and <u>Lebanon</u> shall be turned into a <u>fruitful field</u>. And the fruitful field shall be esteemed as a forest? And in <u>that day</u> shall <u>the deaf hear the words of the book</u>, and the <u>eyes</u> of the <u>blind</u> shall also <u>see out of obscurity</u>, and <u>out of darkness</u>. The <u>meek</u> also shall <u>increase</u> their <u>joy</u> in the <u>Lord</u>, and the <u>poor among men</u> shall <u>rejoice</u> in the <u>Holy One</u> of <u>Israel</u>. For the <u>Terrible one</u> is <u>brought to naught</u>, and the <u>scorner</u> is <u>consumed</u>, and <u>All that watch</u> for <u>iniquity</u> are <u>cut off</u>: That <u>make a man</u> an <u>offender</u> for a <u>word</u>, and <u>lay</u> a <u>snare</u> for <u>him</u> that <u>Reproveth</u> in the <u>gate</u>, and <u>turn aside</u> the <u>just</u> for a thing of naught. This meaning that in the Last Days, the sealed book of Revelation shall begin to be understood, then shall the God of the Earth come-forth in Spirit, which is only to say a terrible event comes unto the earth which shall cause the earth to move out of its place and many shall die and great nations shall fall and rise not again. And another shall come and by that coming many shall loose Faith of Christ Jesus and receive a strange God, even the God of the Earth. Let me explain: Again in the Last Days, when the book of Revelation is opened and the deaf and blind begin to hear and understand, which is even Now, what must follow is he who desires to take it away. And he truly comes and even Now is the way being made. Yet, before he Reveals himself, Knowledge of God's Word must increase as it is done, and also the Knowledge of the World likewise. To this cause shall the Wisdom of their Wise men perish. Indeed, things shall be turned upside down. Yet in this hour God has poured out His Spirit unto All flesh and His Knowledge, to say in His house, has been increased and many shall enter in the Holy Place, Christ Jesus, And the Rapture is come. To this cause say I unto you, go not back into your house to gather things unto yourself, but rather enter into the Holy Place. For those who see Son of Man coming in the clouds of*

Heaven are they of the Rapture for they discern the times and the seasons and enter in. Yet they that see not, shall not know that day and the God of the Earth shall they see. For I tell you a Truth, they that return to go into their house will lose site of the Lord and will remain to behold the God of the Earth. Therefore pray unto your souls that your flight be not in the Winter (the Last Days) or on the Sabbath (days of Christ). For I tell you a Truth, because each is a Death and a Resurrection, they are likened one to the other. The First Resurrection ends after a thousand year Reign of Christ, which its end is seen by the bottomless pit being opened which causes an increase in Worldly Knowledge, that is to say, he Satan begins to deceive the Nations. And this occurs in the fifth trumpet, meaning that during the thousand year Reign of Christ four (4) of the trumpets took place and therefore there was not peace on the earth while Christ and those with Him were in peace. For these things were done in spirit and therefore not seen of men. Yet you can find His peace for it is in you. Yea, the Kingdom of God is within you. Even so Father.

Amen.......

Now, because time does not stop at the Rapture, which is of the Second Resurrection, the time of the God of the Earth begins. And they that remain are the Last that might glorify the God of Heaven and be saved. Now consider what Christ said of the servant who knew the will of his Lord and prepared not himself, that he would be whipped of many stripes before he would enter into the Kingdom of God. So that All of God's words might be fulfilled, has this strange work of God come to be. Even in the time of the Two (2) Witnesses who are prepared of the Father. And shall show many wonders unto the seed of Cain. But first the Rapture and the falling away or the Revealing of this One of Greatness. Who comes in All Lying Wonders and signs whose works are after Satan. For while he was in Heaven he dwelt in High Places and likewise in the Earth he dwells in High Places. To this cause in the Last days he the God of the Earth shall Transform Himself into an Angel of Light and be Revealed. Yet, nevertheless the God of Heaven shall punish him. As it is written in Isaiah 24:21 ; And it shall come to pass in that day, that the Lord shall punish the host of the High Ones that are on high, and the Kings of the Earth upon the earth. It is written in this manner because as the kings upon the earth sit in High Places so also do these spirits sit in High Places upon or in the earth in this the Last Days. And to this cause shall the Two Witnesses stand before the God of the Earth. And after this shall the end come. Let every man who has an ear hear and understand what the Spirit of Truth says: In the beginning of days, even the time of old when those of Renown walked in the Lands. They found themselves wise because of their places and knew not the One who is unseen. Yea, this One who has made us the same is He who is unseen. He has taken on being the Not, that All and All might be. Now the wise and prudent know of the High Places, but the Power therein is not theirs to give. For when they were called they would not listen and what they had was taken away. This was so in its beginning so shall it be in its end. Yea, they were moved from the High Places in Heaven and so shall it be on the Earth in the Last Days. O, Inhabitance of the Earth, weep Exceedingly, even unto thy soul. For the terrible day of the Lord is Nigh before you and the time of the deceitful one is even now in your mouth. Yea, his

33

name is a lie and he comes in it to transform into His Great Light. Indeed, the remainder of the Earth shall receive him and he will destroy them with his false peace. Yet there are two (2) who shall know him and stand against the God of the Earth. The Earth shall be moved exceedingly and Great Heat shall be the breath which prepares he who comes forth in spirit even as he who returns in Silence. Behold the time has come that the Earth must be burned to prepare the way, Behold the God of the Earth is come! Shall He save the Earth and become the Liar? Children, Enter into the Holy Place (Christ). He Abides Always, He never Leaves you, so discern the times and season and Enter in. His Voice, you are in Him, think not that you would not find Him as He calls in this that day. Behold a burning Light approaches. It is from the Altar and the Angel of Fire has cast it down. Yea, the way of the old one is made and the Seal of Silence is broken away. The Great Ones are now Revealed . Who will He not persuade. Oh, Children with the Faith of Christ, hold on to that which you have. For there is One who comes to take it from you with a crown of false glory and a Power that shall surely deceive the World which for a short season will yet remain. Even so Oh Lord

Amen.......

Thank three oh Father thy Holy Spirit is forever with us and thy servant John is heard by every creature which is in Heaven, and on the earth, and under the earth, and such as are in the sea and all that are in them. And thy servant John is heard praising God in this thy Glorious Day. Oh hear me all my fellow-servants and know the Mystery of this Revelation the Lord Jesus Christ gave my portion to be. For the foundation of the earth, which Our Lord passed through are the hundred and forty-four thousand (144,000) sealed by the Ascending Angel from the east, which is Christ arisen. And the twelve (12) for which John is apart that are in Him, the same are the Elect. From the time of the prophets, even as John's hand passed (translated) it is, the First Resurrection, from which John is made the last of the foundation of the Church. For the hundred and forty-four thousand (144,000) were unto God the First Fruits and given unto the Lamb and they followed the Lamb withersoever He goeth. Now the three days that Christ was in the foundation of the earth, He sealed or received these unto Himself, for Mount Sion is the foundation of the earth. And the Lord God Almighty gave His First Fruits unto the Lamb, to make war with the great dragon that old serpent, called the Devil, and Satan. And he was cast out of Heaven "into" the earth and his angels with him. Consider this; Jesus said unto His disciples when one of them drew his sword and struck a servant of the high priests: Put up again thy sword into his place: for all they that take the sword shall perish with the sword. Thinkest thou that I can not now pray to My <u>Father</u>, and He shall presently <u>give me</u> more than <u>twelve Legions</u> of <u>Angels</u>? For the Son knoweth what the Father hath given Him. Now here is the patience of the Saints: For they the twelve (12) are the first of the remnant which came-forth from the First Fruits, which is the First Resurrection. And some of the first shall be last and the last shall be first. Now to say the twelve (12) are the first of the remnant of the hundred and forty-four thousand (144,000) is because the twelve sang the "New Song". For which only the hundred and forty-four thousand (144,000) and the remnant could learn. Let me explain; To say remnant is to show that they upon the earth draw life from the Spirit. Either from above or from below. As Jesus said: I Am from above and you are from below. I hear and say of My Father, and you of yours. You know not of Me or My Father, for your father is the Devil and there is no truth in him. For if you knew My Father, you would know Me: This is only to say that the twelve (12) came-forth out of the First Fruits, hundred and forty-four thousand (144,000), which were Redeemed from among men and they the twelve (12) were born again. Not born of flesh, but of Spirit. For their spirit and their soul were united (Sealed) by the Power of God and the Lamb. And they being the first of men to enter into the Kingdom of Heaven. It is by this Truth that they the twelve (12) were able to speak of Heavenly things. Consider this: As it is written in Revelation 19:1, And after these things I heard a great voice of _much people_, in Heaven, saying Alleluia; Salvation, and Glory and Honour and Power unto the Lord Our God; For these are they of the First Resurrection, yet they came not out of Great Tribulation, but are they which are called unto the Marriage Supper of the Lamb. As it is written in Revelation 19:6, And I heard as it were the voice of a _great multitude_, and as the voice of _many waters_, and as the voice of thunderings saying Alleluia: For the Lord God Omnipotent reignth. Let us be glad and rejoice, and give honour to Him: for the Marriage of the Lamb is come, and His wife (Church) hath made herself ready. And to her was granted that she should be arrayed in fine Linen, clean and white: for fine Linen is the Righteousness of Saints. Let me further explain; The twelve (12) are they that are servants of God gathering together All who are called unto the Marriage Supper of the Lamb, which is the First Resurrection. And they that are upon the earth in this that day, were and are the remnant for which the Harvest was Great . As Jesus said: The harvest truly is Great, but the Laborers are few: Pray ye therefore the Lord of the Harvest, that He would send forth laborers into His harvest. To this end do I tell you that the great multitude (Revelation 19:6) that were in Heaven was during the First Resurrection when the twelve (12) disciples began to call the great multitude unto the Marriage Supper of the Lamb. They being the first of the First Resurrection which after the Marriage of the Lamb it remained a thousand (1,000) years. So also do I tell you that the Great Multitude (Revelation 7:9), which no man could number, of All nations and Kindreds and peoples and tongues, that stood before the throne, and before the Lamb, clothed with white robes, and palms in their hands, that their remnant are the same generation that walk in this very day, which came forth out of Great Tribulation.. For this same remnant walk on the earth this day of the Second Resurrection, even the Last Generation. For which _we_ are that remnant. And indeed _we_ are of the _Last Generation_. When the Second Resurrection is complete _our_ Soul and _our_ Spirit shall be united (Sealed) unto everlasting habitation. Seek then therefore unto yourselves the fruit of the Holy Spirit, that you might take on This Glory and This Likeness and be children of Light. To whom it is given, let him receive it. For I tell you a Great Truth: He who has come among you in this Last hour of Redemption is the Father. Do not marvel over this, but rather understand. For he who was first, the same is the Father of All flesh. The first Adam, and the second Adam, was and is the Son of Man. For that which was Lost through the First Adam, was and is saved by the Son of Man, the second Adam. And he who was first shall be last and for this reason Adam the Father of All *flesh must be last to come and the Son of Man the First. And He who has no name, but God Almighty, the Father of All Creation. It is He "Alone" that sets on the <u>Great White Throne</u>, from whose face the earth and heaven fled away: And there was found no place for them. Know then that this one who has come among us in this the Last Days, has come in Spirit and dwells in the hearts of men who do <u>Good</u> <u>Works</u>, not for themselves, but for the sake of Good Itself, which is the Lord's doing and it is marvelous unto our sight. And these men are the remnant of they which come out of Great Tabulation, and have washed their robes, and made them white in the blood of the Lamb. Therefore are they before the Throne of God, and serve Him day and night in His temple. They that believe and hold fast onto the Truth and faint not (be not offended) the same wash their robes in the blood of the Lamb. His temple being man (remnant) and day and night is to say during the Resurrection. For after the Resurrection God the Father of Creation, shall create "A New". And there shall be no night in Heaven, only day and the Lamb shall be the Light of it. Consider this: I tell you a Truth: if a man should make the tree good, the fruit thereof shall be likewise. And if the fruit is good, then his soul and spirit are one and his Angel (soul) stands before God in Heaven. And if this man should go through Great Tribulation his soul being one with him, shall Keep him and he will not faint, but endure. Now if this man should make the tree evil, will not the fruit be the same? And if the fruit is evil, then is not his soul before the God of the earth? And if Great Tribulation should come unto the man, how shall he stand and who shall comfort him? How then can a man make the tree good or evil? What shall a man believe? And what shall he live, but that which he believes! Take hold of the Truth and the Truth is God. Yet, no man has seen Him, but the Son of God. Therefore, believe on Him and be like-minded. And this is being like-minded: Do good unto others and be not offended if they return not good unto you, but rather use you. Be glad and rejoice for your Father in Heaven shall reward you. And if a man should hurt you: seek not to do the same, but rather forgive him and your Father in Heaven shall forgive you likewise. It is in this reasoning that you might make the tree <u>Good</u> or <u>Evil</u>. If you can believe this Truth and seek to Live it. Know also that this One who judges shall come unto you and measure this against you. Therefore, hold fast unto the Lord and His Grace and you shall endure. Oh Praise thee Father for thy Beloved Son. For it is in thy Righteousness that we might be Redeemed unto thy Holiness. Even so Father.*

Amen.... and Amen.......

And concerning the Resurrection; as it is written in Revelation 7:16 . They shall hunger no more, neither thirst any more: neither shall the sun light on them, nor any heat. For the Lamb which is in the midst of the throne shall <u>feed</u> them, and shall <u>lead</u> them unto <u>Living</u> fountains of <u>waters</u>: This is only to say that again man is God's temple and these are they that dwell in men, that shine forth the Light of their Heavenly Father. And for this cause they shall not hunger nor thirst anymore, neither shall the sun light on them, nor any heat. And because the Second Resurrection is not yet complete, the Lamb shall <u>lead</u> them unto <u>Living</u> fountains of <u>waters</u>. For when the Second Resurrection is accomplished they shall All <u>freely Drink</u> from <u>Living waters</u>, as they <u>will</u>. For each shall be a "true" Son of God.

Let not misunderstandings come from these sayings, because not all men have Light, but rather darkness that shine forth out of them. And to some the darkness is Great. For each is worthy of his hire. And for this cause has God the Father of Creation allowed each to be and they shall fulfill His purpose. And to this do I say: Oh children of darkness, whose portion is among the unbelievers. Your time has come before you, and your fear and anger are made Great. You go now in the way of your father, even until God Almighty, His words are fulfilled. In the foundation of the earth did you make war and in the Remnant shall you do the same. Glory to God the Father, it is in His Power, which gave you a short season to reign. And the blood that you have shed, the same has Our Lord Christ taken and washed us clean. Now that you have waxed Great, even of the number of which is as the sand of the sea. Have you not gone up on the breadth of the earth? Even as your King Abandon has commanded you, and gathered together the Kings of the earth, and chief captains, and the mighty men, that you might know of their flesh. And have you not become two fold the children of your King? Woe, Woe, Woe unto you by reason of the truth. Woe unto you, because you know not the Joy of Love and the Power and Strength of it. For Love contains Forgiveness, Mercy, Patience, Long-sufferings,Compassion, Goodness, Meekness, Gentleness, Faithfulness for which you can not Know because you can not find a Trust of Love in you. For without Love there can be no peace or rest in you, but fear that one greater then yourself might come and take that which is yours away from you. Therefore, fear shall become your eye and deceitfulness your ear. Woe unto you, because you have no part of Truth in you. Therefore, how will you know he who lies to you is the Father of Lies? And that he teaches you the ways of damnation and he calls it righteousness. For he desires his church and his disciples of it. For he lust to be worshipped. And his Joy and Love is to continually show his destructive power, which is made of Hate, Anger, Deceitfulness, Revenge, Hostility and Death. Woe unto you, because there are those among you who will hear these things and Know they are True and part from you. For it was because of your deceitfulness that they followed you and because you are not able to understand these things you will not have the power to go with them, but rather you shall remain by the power of your offense and hatred. For you know not the God of Truth and will not call on His Name. Therefore, your anger and wrath will be stirred-up and it shall be turned onto you and your torment shall be made an hundred (100) fold and be everlasting. For Just and Righteous is the Lord God of Creation. And it is He Himself that has sacrificed a part of Himself so that All things were and are created. And those that say there is no Hell, let him search the Scriptures for God created All things, even an Evil One. For a purpose which only God and His Elect Know and to whom He will reveal it unto. For this Evil One, the same is he which was, and is not, but yet is. For I tell you a Truth, the day comes and even now is before you that you shall behold this One and shall pray for God to return him unto Hell, which has become the "Lake of Fire" forever and ever.

Amen !..

For I tell you a Truth: they who say there is not a Hell is bound for it and knows not where they are. As Jesus said; fear not those who can only kill your body, but fear He who can destroy your body and soul in Hell! This I say again, God the Father of Creation Gave of Himself, which means He sacrificed of Himself and that which is given is indeed sacrificed!! Know you not that the Altar is built for fire? That the sacrifice is burned? Are you that part of Him, He shall sacrifice and burn? Or shall you be that part of Him, He shall raise-up and make "New"? Consider this; In Revelation 20:11, And I saw a Great White Throne, and Him that set on it, from whose face the earth and the heaven fled away; and there was found no place for them. Yet there is a place called "Lake of Fire", even when the earth and the heaven are no more because there is no place for them, the"Lake of Fire" shall be forever and ever burning. Then shall God create a new heaven and earth. Amen... Even as God created Evil, He created a place for it. Consider this; the parable of Lazarus and the rich man, and how the rich man received of good things in his lifetime and Lazarus evil things. And how when Lazarus <u>died</u> the <u>Angels carried</u> him into <u>Abraham's bosom</u>, but the rich man who also <u>died</u>, he was <u>buried</u>. The meaning is this, the beggar (Lazarus) was put before the rich man so that he (the rich man) might take the good things of his lifetime and give, even as it was given unto him. But he not understanding, would fare sumptuously everyday and not give Alms of that which he had. For this cause he was buried in deceitfulness of riches. And in his death found the torment of such flames. Yet he was able to see afar off. Even unto Abraham's bosom. And to speak to him, also to hear, so that he might understand. Here is the faithfulness of true heart: if this rich man were of no good at all, he would have anger and revenge to God by reason of his torments. Yet he found in himself Love enough to consider his five (5) brethren in his father's house. That they might not come into this place of torment. What then of Abraham's answer to the rich man? Where is God's Mercy and Compassion? Does not this one in hell have yet some Love in himself? Indeed so, and to this cause are there two (2) Resurrections. And also the reason why Abraham answered him as he did concerning the Great Gulf Fixed between them. For after the thousand (1000) years expires in the First Resurrection the dead (buried) shall live again. And for this reason Lazarus was not sent unto the five (5) brethren, because God's ways are sufficient to save all that is Lost. And if you are one who Judges God and says; How could God let one suffer in torment for a thousand years. It is not good for one to Judge God, but rather trust your Creator! But to show such a one God's Mercy and Compassion, hear this; a thousand years unto us is but a moment to God and Spirit. Is it evil that a father teach his blind son of fire by touch so that he would not be consumed in the learning? For it is not the will of the Heavenly Father that even one of these Little Ones should perish. Since the time of Eve, there have been many who by this deceitful One, have entered into this place of torment. Not because they are deceitful, but rather they have been deceived. For this Evil Spirit was created to be a Great Power, because God Almighty is Great and He desires to Judge Himself. To this cause there are those that are Lost, that they might become witnesses unto God's purpose. Even as Christ was made Lesser of Heaven that He might know the Greater of it. This is also why Abraham said; they would not be persuaded though One rose from the *dead. For those that are truly deceitful will remain so even if they are raised-up again from their place of habitation. Yet those which were deceived, if they are raised-up again, they shall hear the Truth and it will become their eye and ear and their heart shall understand. For God's Grace is the Power of Faith. And Faith comes from hearing and hearing from the Word of God. For in the beginning of deception Eve was told that should she partake of the forbidden fruit, she would become as God. Which is only to say, she would be able to know the difference between good and evil (which is understanding of All and All). That she could make herself Good, even as God is Good. My friends, hear the Truth; There are those who believe if they should gain understanding of All things, they will find Salvation. It Is Not So! For Salvation comes from Faith of God's Promise and likewise understanding. It is not possible that a man can know All and All. Least there would be no need of the Creator. The Truth is, there is no need for man. For God is All and All. Yet God desires man to be by reason of His Love. This is not His weakness, but rather His strength. For Love is sufficient unto Love. Even as Grace is sufficient unto Forgiveness. Indeed, it is through Love All things are created, even Evil. For the accuser said unto God; Your Love is your weakness and it shall overtake You! Even as Jesus said; And from the days of John the Baptist until now the Kingdom of Heaven suffered violence, and the violent take it by force. Meaning this Accuser believed he could take heaven from God, by using God's Love against Himself. Therefore this Accuser Judged God's Love and God's Love overcame the Accuser. This being the purpose God created this Evil One. That He might judge His Love and it endure. Out of Love God created all things. Even this Evil One. Please do not misunderstand these sayings. This is the greater cause, but not the only one for God to create an Evil One. And remember this; when the Shining One was created he was in his beginning perfect in wisdom and beauty. And again I say, only God's Faith brings Salvation. For it was from Faith that Adam named All things God brought before him. For God gave this understanding unto Adam in it's due season. Indeed, for it was not Adam who went out to seek the understanding of these things. For Adam's knowledge came not from self, but from Faith which came from God the Father of Creation. For All things were and are created by reason of God's Faith. I tell you a Truth, only God the Father of Creation can understand All and All. And only in Faith and Patience can man receive true knowledge and wisdom. For knowledge is nothing without wisdom. For if a man should have knowledge and no wisdom, he will use it wrongly and find only fault and error in his works. Yet if he should have wisdom, he will be patient and the knowledge will be revealed unto him in it's due season. And he would use the knowledge wisely, and the works thereof shall be good and no fault shall become of it. Not in this day, nor the days to follow. Even so Father.*

Amen and Amen........

And as to touching knowledge, patience, and wisdom, God gave us the knowledge of His works in the Spirit of Prophecy, which is Jesus Christ. And through the Saints we might learn patience, which brings wisdom and through wisdom we might begin to understand what season is upon us and return unto Faith and Praise God. For it is through Faith, not man's reasoning, that we will begin to understand the meaning of the prophecies of Revelation. To this end do I say unto All of you who might hear. Take hold of Faith, which is foolishness in the <u>eyes</u> of the <u>world</u>. Yet, <u>wisdom</u> in the <u>eye</u> of Our <u>Lord</u>. Now as to the prophecies of Revelation, consider this; Jesus said unto the twelve (12) disciples, that there shall be twelve (12) thrones to judge the twelve (12) tribes of the children of Israel. And in Revelation it is written that he (John) saw thrones, and <u>they</u> sat upon them, and <u>judgment</u> was given unto <u>them</u>. This being the twelve (12) thrones Jesus spoke about unto the twelve (12) disciples, which is of the First Resurrection. For the First Resurrection began with Christ Jesus and ends after the twelve (12) throne judgment is finished and the thousand (1,000) years expired. There are some who say; the thousand (1,000) years shall be of peace on earth, but it is not so. Those that are of peace, the same are the souls that were beheaded for the witness of Jesus, and for the Word of God. Also they to whom judgment was given. To say they on the judgment thrones. And then the Nations would not be deceived by Satan for a thousand (1,000) years. This does not say the earth shall have peace. Only that Satan would not be able to deceive the Nations. Do you not yet understand? Even as Christ said, it is so. He said: Woe unto the world for offenses, but the world needs offenses. Look not for heaven on earth! It is not to be. Least God would not have heaven and earth flee from His Face and there was no place found for them. And also He would have no need to create a <u>New Heaven</u> and <u>Earth</u>. Deceive not yourselves. Now the Marriage of the Lamb is in the midst of the First Resurrection for which the twelve (12) Apostles' are a part. This being so because the twelve (12) are the foundation of the Church. And the church being the <u>Wife</u> of the <u>Lamb</u>. As it is written in Revelation 19:7, Let us be glad and rejoice and give Honour to Him for the Marriage of the Lamb <u>is come</u>, and His <u>Wife</u> has <u>made herself ready</u>. This meaning that All of the twelve (12) have been translated into Heaven. This also being the time the Vials begin. This being so because once the vials begin No Man may enter into the Temple of God until they (the vials) are completed. Therefore, the vials did not start until after the twelve (12) were translated into the Kingdom of God. Or how else could they speak Heavenly Things. Yet the twelve throne judgment had not yet begun, because the Beast and the False Prophet are cast into the Lake of Fire before the twelve (12) throne judgment begins. But not before the sixth vial is poured out. Therefore know that the vials were accomplished in the First Resurrection and therefore finished. Yet there are those who believe the world shall have a thousand (1,000) years of peace and that those Redeemed from the earth shall reign on the earth during this thousand (1,000) years. Hear and understand; the thousand (1,000) years of peace is for those who shall dwell with Christ and He dwells in Heaven, not on the earth. As Jesus said unto His <u>disciples</u>; I <u>go</u> to <u>prepare</u> a <u>place</u> for <u>you</u>. And if I go and <u>prepare</u> a <u>place</u> for <u>you</u>, I will <u>come again</u>. And <u>receive you unto myself</u>; that <u>where</u>

I am, there *ye may be also*. Jesus also said where this place would be. In *My Father's House* are many *Mansions*. That is to say the Kingdom of God (Heaven). It is a thousand (1,000) years of peace for those Received of the First Resurrection and also a thousand (1,000) years that the world would not be Deceived by this Evil One. Which is only to say that the world's *foolish knowledge* would *not increase* until He (the *Evil One*) was *released* for a *short season*. And as for those who say Christ shall return and dwell on the earth, Believe them Not! For He returns to receive unto Himself that which is His. As it is written in Thessalonians 1 4:16, For the *Lord Himself* shall *descend* from *Heaven* with a *shout*, with the *voice* of the *Archangel*, and with the *trump* of *God*: And the *dead* in Christ shall *rise first*. *Then we* which *are Alive* and *remain shall be caught up* together with them *in* the *clouds* to *meet* the *Lord in the air*: And so shall we ever be with the Lord. My friends, let not the world's foolishness deceive you. Consider what Jesus said unto His disciples: Yet a little while and the *world seeth Me* "*No more*"; but ye see Me: because I Live, ye shall Live also: *He that hath My Commandments*, and *keepth them, he it is that Loveth Me* and *he that Loveth Me shall be Loved of My Father, and I will Love him* and *manifest Myself to him*. This is only to say that Christ shall not return to dwell upon the earth. For He comes in Spirit to receive Spirit. And here is the Wisdom of the Saints: What manner of man can see an angel? If a man is in the Spirit, will he not be able to see Spirit? Therefore know how to watch so that you might see. For the dead in Christ are in Him who is "Alive". Therefore they are dead yet alive and shall Hear His voice and be raised- up in the Last Days. For he who is first shall be last, and the last shall be first. Now in the Last Days, they (remnant) who are of course the last ones to receive Him, and there are those who taste not death until the Lord Christ returns in Spirit. These are the same who were first to receive Him and remain. They also being the last to be taken up, but the first to be *called by His voice.* Yet those Alive in Christ, who hear Him, shall speak among men, because these men are dead in Christ and shall be raised up first into the clouds and they who are Alive in Christ shall follow after them and together meet the Lord in the air. And so shall we ever be with the Lord. And therefore as it was in the former days (days of Christ), so shall it be in the latter days (Two Witnesses). Even so Father, thy Works have Honoured Thee.

Amen and Amen.......

Therefore, my friends, (and they who are my friends, they do know me), know the meaning of this saying; there are those who are first and therefore last, and the last shall be first. And also I give unto you another Mystery. In the sixth (6) trumpet, the Angel with the little book in his hand, who stands his right foot on the sea and his left foot on the earth. And He *sware by Him* that *Lives forever* and *ever*, that there *should be time no longer*. He is of the sixth (6) and not the seventh (7). Therefore howbeit that there is time for the seventh (7) trump, when it *should end* at the sixth (6) *who sware by Him* that *Lives forever* and *ever*, that it *should end*? And this I tell you so that you might have some understanding. In the time of the sixth (6) trump, the two (2) witnesses shall prophesy, and at the end of their testimony, shall be taken

41

up, and there are _those_ (remnant) who were _affrighted_ and _gave_ _God_ of _Heaven_ _Glory_. These are the same who are _last_ being saved. This meaning, the _time for being saved_ (received) has _ended_, yet _time on earth_ shall _continue_ for a _short space_, for the third (3) Woe comes quickly. Now when the seventh (7) trump begins, the Nations shall become angry. This again saying, that time on earth continues after the sixth (6) trump ends time for those who are received. Yet, the Nations are angry and not knowing that they have left unseen, the end of being received (Redeemed). Unable to know that the last Resurrection was before them and they would not receive it. For after it, comes then the Great White Throne Judgment, and they upon the earth, in the time of the seventh (7) trump shall reflect it. And in this Judgment, shall the heaven and the earth flee away. It is in this that they of the earth, in the time of the seventh (7) trump shall see. And this indeed is a Great Woe. For I tell you a Truth: the first Woe has already come unto you, and the second is being prepared. Even at the door. For the time of the seven (7) thunders has begun. And they shall utter their voices, but of them shall two (2) turn away. For the seven (7) thunders are the seven (7) great churches of the Last Days. For one is being prepared to die, and the other knows not that he is dead and savors death in his works. For they are the son of perdition, and shall enter therein. Marvel not that _they_ are the _Son_ of perdition, for the two (2) are one. Even as Adam and Eve are one. Consider Genesis 5:2, male and female created He _them_, and blessed _them_, and called _their name_ _Adam_, in the day when _they_ were created. Let not this saying trouble you. For the son of perdition has a beginning, and an end and each are a son, yet they are one in their cause. It is also asked, why is he a part of the seven? And I say unto you; even as he was part of the twelve. Likewise has he entered into the seven. For God has given him Great Authority from the beginning of days, because he is the _Cherub_ who _Covers_ and he shall exercise the same. Then you shall ask: Why are there two (2) and why is one prepared to die, and the other knows not? Truly I say unto you; He who is prepared to die, the same is that which was given, that the Son of God shall be as His Father. Which is only to say, as the Father has given of Himself, so also has the Son given of Himself. Yet the Father, raised up the Son, who was given for many. Likewise, the Son of God shall raise up in the Last days, that which was given Him of the Father. To this cause is this one prepared to die to strengthen that which remains. That God's words might be fulfilled; the sacrifice and the sacrificer are one. For as the Father gave so that the Son might be. So also has the Son given, so that we might be. Which is only to say, so God and Man shall walk as one. Even so Oh Holy One

Amen.......

And to this one that knows not that he is dead, Satan, the same is he who God the Father of Creation, gave and truly he is given to everlasting damnation. He is not to be destroyed, but rather shall be cast into utter darkness, where He shall never enter into Life again, and this is His everlasting torment, because of the Great Gulf Fixed, which will allow him to see and hear, but not to touch or enter into again the things of Life.

Amen and Amen!!!

Now there are those who say you can not have that which burns forever. Have you not read of the burning bush that was not consumed? Do you not know that the power of Almighty God is <u>Limitless</u>? If you know not this, then surely you are marked among men, and that which you receive here in this your life is your reward, and your only life. Least at any time you should call on the Name of the Lord and believe on Him and His Works. Therefore, love your enemies (those who persecute you, and use you). To love your enemies is to forgive them and hold them not responsible for their offenses, but rather hold responsible this One, who is Evil. Likewise there is One responsible for Righteousness for whom God the Father of Creation made and He is Lord. And God the Father of Creation is Lord over Him. That is to say, Lord of my Lord. As Jesus said; But be ye not called Rabbi: for one is your Master, <u>even</u> (also) <u>Christ</u>; and <u>All ye Are Brethren</u>. And call no man your Father (Lord) upon the earth: for one is your Father (Lord), which is in Heaven.. Neither be ye called Master: for one is your Master, even (also) Christ. But he that is greatest among you shall be your servant. In this saying many have misunderstood Jesus the man. For Jesus the man said that the things he spoke were not his words, but the Father's, and that if you are able to receive him (Jesus) then you were also receiving the Father (He who sent Him). Jesus said that man was the temple of God. He also said: And whosoever shall sware by the temple, swareth by it, and by <u>him that dwelleth therein</u>. This is to say: Man is the temple of God and that which dwells within can be Good or Evil. To this cause did Jesus say: Make the tree good or make the tree evil. And the tree is make good or evil, by reason of the fruit. And the fruit is made by reason of the light of the eye, and the eye is the lamp of the body. Howbeit, that I speak of a tree and of a body likewise? The tree is the beliefs or concepts a man is able to live, and how he lives will determine the fruit of his labour. For the light of the eye will make the fruit, and the fruit shall reveal the tree and the tree shall become that which the eye is able to see and if the eye be single, then the whole body is single and the light thereof likewise. Therefore there is no sin in him. Behold, he is made clean. And if the eye is not single the body is full of darkness. And how great is that darkness? The fruit thereof shall reveal the tree and the evil therein shall make it desolate and it must surely pass away. Therefore let the light of the eye be single. Which is only to say, judge not your brother, but rather love him and if you must judge let your judgment be this: There is not One Good man, no not one. For only One is Good, The Heavenly Father. Therefore let His Light shine forth from you and Glorify Him in it. Truly I say unto you, if any man should display good works, Let him know that the Lord has flowed through him. For this judgment is true and came forth from our Lord Christ. Even so Holy Father

Amen and Amen.......

The six days of Creation is the Regeneration of time and the seventh day of creation is the Regeneration of Man as Lord to <u>come</u> by reason of Son of Man, who is Lord of the Sabbath, which is the Seventh day of Creation As it is written in Genesis, on the seventh day the Lord rested from the work which He <u>made</u>. And sanctified it and made it Holy (gave it purpose).

43

Man is a part of God, as all things. Yet man is a part which <u>died</u>.. Man has always been a part of God, but man has not always walked one with Him. God has chosen man to be Lord of the Creation. This is the Regeneration of Son of Man. To say man as Lord and God dwelling in him. Christ is the First and the Last of All Sons of God (Lords of Creation). This which I am saying is that Man was in God's purpose to die. This being, so God could pick up (Regenerate) and dwell in him and becoming One (Lord of Creation, Sons of God). When God took the dust and made man, this is only to say He remembered him (Regeneration). And when He gave Life to him and made him a Living Soul, He gave Him "purpose" for being <u>everlasting</u>. Yet, man has a beginning, because he is <u>as</u> God, but not Him. Therefore man must have a beginning though God has chosen to make him with no End.. For God has No beginning nor No end. Yet the Son of God who <u>Is</u> The Mystery of the Creation of God.. Therefore the Son of God has given God that which He had not before, which is a beginning and to this end has God done the impossible again, because in the Beginning when God Created All Things, He First made Himself <u>Not</u> so that All and All Might Be. To this cause has <u>No</u> <u>one</u> <u>ever</u> <u>seen</u> <u>God</u> nor His shape. Not even the Host of Heaven. Yet The Son Knows Him, nevertheless, man being made Lord by reason of God's Elect, has a beginning and shall be transformed into no end. Now because man has a beginning, he must reach an end. Then be Resurrected, this being the transformation or Regeneration of Son of Man then mankind. Therefore know that the end must come so that the Everlasting shall take on form to its being, that has No end. To this cause have we become as God, but not Him. Which is to say Sons of God the Father of Creation. For the Sons of God have a beginning, even as God Created, and because they are Sons of God, they have No end, even as God is without End. For they are as Him. God has Begotten but One Son and through Him (Christ), many have come forth, even as God created one man (Adam) and many have come forth. To this cause do I say unto you that on the day that Jesus was crucified on the tree and said; "It is Finished", this was the end of the sixth day and the beginning of the seventh day of creation. For on the seventh day God Rested from the work which He had made and His Only Begotten Son became Lord of the Sabbath and received All things unto Himself. For God has made Him (Christ) Lord of Heaven and Earth and this man child was caught up unto God's Throne, meaning on that day God had begotten Him. Jesus was begotten on the Seventh day and to this cause He was, is, and will be Holy. Which is only to say, Forever and Ever He is Holy. Even so Father.

Amen and Amen.......

To the man of logic of this world who is governed by the Spirit of Pride in Self Achievement, whose confidence is in his vain Accomplishments of <u>dead</u> works which shall surely pass away. Hear this oh fearful man of No Faith. Whose foolish trust of Darkness called logic leads himself into the pit of Utter Darkness which shall become forever and ever from the presence of the Lord.The Holy Spirit is that which is Needed and Not the Knowledge which the Logic of the world shall surely bring. For the Knowledge of the world brings A Great City that shortly in Its coming Must have a Great Fall. Seek not the Knowledge of the False High

Ones, whose Knowledge is made into Nothing by the Power of God Almighty, which is the Works of the Holy Spirit. For He speaks not His own, but that which He hears. Oh fearful man who desires to Know Faith turn your ear unto the Holy Spirit and He will show you that which the Lord has written in your Heart that you might Know it also in your mind. He the Holy Spirit teaches the things you need even in the hour that you need; the same is the Knowledge which He shall bring. Let this be your understanding and your wisdom shall be the Knowledge of the Father and the Son and you shall be One in the Holy Spirit and He will teach the world of Repentance for we have All sinned, and teach of Righteousness, for the Lord returned to the Father. and we must learn to believe on Him, and teach of Judgment for the prince of the world has been judged, and we must learn of this Judgment. Therefore the High Ones must come that we might learn of the beasts of the world which are the Nations these High Ones do lead, even in the day that they are Revealed. For they are masters in their Knowledge, for it is their portion and their reward given from the Father in the beginning of days. Yet they know not the Creator, And His Holy Spirit they do not hear. For this worldly Knowledge is All that they trust and the Faith and Patience of the Holy Spirit is foolishness unto their ears. Now learn of the hidden truth in the Lord's word of Life in the Son of Man and All that are in Him and also the Son of Darkness and All that are in him. Yea, they are All sons of God, even as All men are sons of Adam. Yet there are two (2) Mysteries in Heaven. One being the birth of the House of God unto men (Church) and that of Iniquity by which man fell into, House of false Knowledge (church) the birth of a Lie. Indeed, you will find each of these sons in mankind. This is so because God in the beginning found a Righteous Purpose to allow such a division to come into being and by this cause did God chose to Judge Himself that this expansion would be found in Heaven. Yea, All men are sons of Adam, even that which entered Adam in the Day Eve was deceived by the serpent. For in that Day was the way made that the serpent and his seed would Once Again become Sons of God. For Iniquity was found in Lucifer's heart. To this cause did the time come that God moved His Spirit Across the face of the deep (death) and the Void, and then came the Mystery of the Image of God as He started His Last Works unto the Creation and did make man. And He who was before man, even the serpent who was sealed unto the tree of the Knowledge of Good and Evil, until the Day that Eve and Adam did eat thereof. And this is the Mystery of Iniquity and how it entered man.. And to this cause is it written; And the Sons of God saw the daughters of men that they were fair; And they took them wives of All which they choose. And Again; There were Giants in the earth in those days; And also after that, when the Sons of God came in unto the daughters of men and they bare children to them, the same became mighty men which were of old, men of Renown. Yea, even the Sons of Iniquity which did corrupt the earth. And God looked upon the earth, and behold, it was corrupt; for All flesh had corrupted his way upon the earth. And once again this Evil One, even a people became Sons of God, even by God's Words (prophesy). As it is written in Ezekiel 28:12 concerning Lucifer; Son of Man, take up a lamentation upon the King Tyrus, and say unto him; (that is to say who dwelled in him), Thus saith the Lord God ; thou sealest

45

up the *sum*, *full* of *wisdom*, and *perfect* in *beauty*. *Thou hast been in Eden the garden of God; every precious stone was thy covering, the Sardius; topaz, and the diamond, the beryl, the onyx and the jasper, the sapphire, the emerald, and the carbuncle, and gold: the workmanship of thy tabrets and of thy pipes was prepared in the day that thou wast created. Thou art the Anointed Cherub that covereth; And I have set thee so: thou wast upon the Holy Mountain of God; thou hast walked up and down in the midst of the stones of fire (that is to say a place called Ermon along the side of the hill, which is the Mountain of God).Thou wast perfect in thy ways from the day that Thou wast created, till iniquity was found in thee. By the multitude of thy Merchandise they have filled the midst of thee with violence, And thou hast sinned: therefore I will cast thee as Profane out of the Mountain of God: And I will destroy thee, O covering cherub, from the midst of the stones of fire. Thine heart was lifted up because of thy beauty, thou hast corrupted thy wisdom by reason of thy brightness: I will cast thee to the ground, I will lay thee before Kings, that they may behold thee.* The word of God as written unto Man in Days of Old, are in part for the events of men and likewise for the Spirits that dwell in him and to this cause did the Spirit of Prophesy come unto Man, As it was in the beginning of Days. For the Lord Rose up early and sent the prophets and the Law and here do we find the hidden Truth of His Prophesies. For the words spoken and thereby written in that Day did speak of things to come in mankind, which would reveal that which is hidden in Him, even the Son of Man and likewise the Son of Iniquity for each do walk in mankind. It is not for us to Judge one another as to who is worthy enough to be a part of Son of Man; for none are worthy in themselves. Have you not read and heard that there is Not One Good Man; No not One. It is True, but there is One who is Good that can be found in us, If you can just believe on Him. And what is believing on Him? To learn of Him and desire to be as Him. That is to say; eat of His Flesh and Drink of His Blood. For if you eat and drink of Him then His Life is found in you. Yet there are those who are "Alive" in Him and also those who are dead in Him. Marvel not at this for did not Our Lord say; and if any man shall believe in Me, though he is dead, yet shall he Live. And again, he who believes in Me receives not Me, but He who sent Me. And again, if any man come unto Me it is because the Father draws him to Me. What this means is this; Only the "few" would be "Alive" in Him. This being shown in their parable of Life and how they would live and by what manner they would be Required of Death. Yet there are many who are saved. Not by Knowledge for it is given unto the few and they walk even this day. For they do Remain and are "Alive", these being the Last to be taken up during the Rapture. Yea, it is not knowledge which is able to save you. To this cause did God allow the Truth to be hidden by this Evil One. For it is given him, to deceive the world by covering up that which was Revealed in the time of Our Lord, even so did the Lord speak in parables so that only with the Spirit of Truth can the wise understand. For God made Salvation a Stumbling block for the wise and prudent (he who trust in Knowledge and not Faith). And a strong Corner Stone for the children. Indeed, God has given the Father and the Son, even the Holy Spirit to make Salvation a sure way unto His children. For He wrote the parable of

Jesus Christ into our hearts and minds that we might desire Him and therefore be like Him and if we are like Him then we will know that Any Good Works found in us is the Father's Works and any True Doctrine found in us is Not our doctrine, but He who has Loved us and sent the Holy One to Redeem us unto God the Father. Nevertheless, there are those who are dead in Christ and to this cause it is not knowledge that will save him, but rather that which God the Father has hidden in him, even in his heart and this is the very works of God made manifest. And as to the Sons of Iniquity; they are not able to find trust in anything except Knowledge and they will use their Knowledge to gain the things of their desire being not concerned of those who might be harmed or hurt by reason of their doings. For they have a mind for self pleasure and a Lust to be Glorified by others who they place under themselves. For their Father is not God, but rather the Prince of the World, and they are like him. This is to say, they shall lift themselves up above men and shall Glorify themselves even before the Lord of Glory. And they shall desire to deceive even the very elect, if it were possible. This meaning that the sayings they bring from their Father are Lies to Confuse many that they (those in the world) might receive this One who comes in All Lying wonders. After the works of Satan. And this is the Revelation of Jesus Christ "Son of Man" concerning the Revelator, "Father of Man". For in the beginning of Days, God the Father of Creation did walk with him (Adam) in the cool of the evening and did prophesy to him concerning the things to come by which None other man would know, save One, "Son of Man". For as God the Father of Creation walked with Adam (Father of Man) so likewise did He walk with Son of Man and to this cause did Jesus say; As I see the Father do, I so do likewise. Nevertheless, in the beginning of Days God "Creator" did prophesy unto Adam and said; you may eat of the trees of the Garden freely, but of the tree of the knowledge of Good and Evil, eat not. <u>For in the Day</u> thou eatest thereof thou shall surely die. Yea, God "Creator" did know that Adam would eat of this tree in due season. To this cause was it said "For <u>in the Day thou eatest thereof</u>", for God "Creator" did <u>Not</u> say; should you eat thereof, but rather <u>when</u> you eat thereof. And again, after God prophesied unto Adam, He continued and said: It is not good that the man should be Alone. Yet, howbeit that Adam could be Alone, when the Father of Creation was within him, even the <u>breath</u> of <u>Life</u>. Again, this work of God "Creator" unto Adam was to prepare for the day that he (Adam) would eat of the forbidden fruit and in dying, he would surely die. For it was not Adam who was deceived by the serpent, but rather Eve the Mother of All Living. Even as Paul said in 1 Timothy 2:14, and Adam was not deceived, but the woman being deceived was in the transgression. This is not to say that Adam did not transgress Against God, but rather that his transgress did not come thru deception from the serpent, because he could not stand before Adam with Authority. Howbeit, that Adam knew him and had Authority over him? Indeed, Adam was not deceived because he walked with God (Creator) and was the very Image of Him. And as the Lord did say in His Generation: The seed must die that many might come forth. Know this also, Son of Man was and is the very Image of the Father. Even as He Himself said; If you see Me, you then see the Father also. For I am in the Father and the Father in Me. Now

47

because Eve, she who came out of Adam, was deceived by the serpent; God (Creator) did promise to glorify her in the passing of Days by the coming of the Lord of Lords and King of Kings through her, even as she came through Adam. Yea, God (Creator) did prophesy unto Adam and Eve, also the serpent when He said; And I will put enmity (hatred and hostility) between thee (serpent) and the woman, and between thy seed and her seed; it (enmity) shall bruise thy head (serpent), and thou shalt bruise his heal (Man). For the bruise was received onto the serpent in the year of our Load, even His generation when He walked among us as a man, even Son of Man. Is it not written in the Gospel that the Lord was tempted of Satan the Devil (serpent) for forty days and nights in the desert? Yea, it is so; And in this that day did the Lord Christ rebuke This High One, even a People and did speak to them in this way; They that be whole need not a Physician, but they that are sick. But go and learn what that meanth, I will have Mercy, and not sacrifice: For I am not come to call the Righteous, but sinners to Repentance. And again, but I say unto you, that in this place is One Greater then the Temple. But if you had known what this meaneth, I will have Mercy, and not sacrifice, ye would not have condemned the guiltless. Indeed, if the wise and prudent had been truly wise, that is to say, hear the Holy Spirit and believe on God's works and not their own, then He the Lord would not have sacrificed. Nevertheless, they could not trust in anything but their Knowledge of the creation and not on Faith which comes from God "Only". For this High One, even a People was hidden in the day of the Lord. And to this day it remains so. Yet an act of God is now before us and shall surly manifest, which shall reveal this High One, even a People. For their Knowledge and Power is Great before men, but not before God. They are even the Fowl of heaven and they desire to be as men, but they are not. Yea, they are man like because of their works and Not by the hand of God and to this cause God has condemned them. Yea, he that comes in his own Name, who has entered into the temple of God to show himself as God. The same has governed the world (the Nations) even before the Lord Christ came into the world. And it was this High One, even a People that tempted the Lord in the desert. But He knew him because the Lord was with God even before the foundation of the world. And to this cause this High One could not deceive Him, even as he could not deceive Adam. For as God said unto Adam, "Because you have harkened unto the voice of your wife"; which is to say he the serpent could not stand before him (Adam) and deceive him.; but did deceive that which came out of Adam, the woman (Eve), Mother of All Living. And Adam, the Father of All flesh so loved Eve that he entered into sin for her and not for himself. Even as the Lord entered into sinful flesh (man) not for Himself, but for many. And did take sin upon Himself for our sake. So is it of Adam, for Eve Is surly the Mother of All Living, even as Adam did say when God brought her before him in the beginning of Days when their Name was called Adam, which is to say One. Now if Eve is the Mother of All Living, then to lose her is to lose All and to save her is to save All. Did not God Judge Himself in the beginning of Days? Or how else could the creation come into being? As long as God considers the Whole of Himself, none of the many parts can be seen because of His Greatness and the Glory and the Light thereof. And likewise, when God considers the

48

part thereof, then the whole can not be seen or else there is no comparison and therefore no Judgment. To this cause did God the Creator hide Himself that the many parts (All and All) could be seen by All and therefore compared and Judged. And this is His Judgment: Even as He is able to hide Himself, for no man has seen Him nor His shape. So shall He hide this Evil One, the Angel of Death and Hell by the Brightness of His Coming, even the Recreation and Regeneration of Son of Man. For in that Day God shall put this One and All that are in him into a Lake of Fire, which shall burn for ever and the Everlasting Kingdom will know him No more. And there will be a New Heaven and a New Earth. For God has cursed this ground for Adam's Sake, which is to say <u>mankind</u> and therefore this Kingdom must pass away and Man must be put into the New Kingdom, even as Adam was put into the Garden of Eden. And so shall it be, because God has taken a sacred oath and has said it. Even so oh Lord.

Amen and Amen.......

For it was God's Words Spoken unto Himself that brought the Creation, even the Beginning of Days. For there was none who stood beside Him.. Therefore only God can hear God's Words. And the things which He Spoke in secret should come to pass. For God desires each part of His Glory to be seen as the whole of His Glory, even as it is written; It is enough that the servant be <u>as his Lord</u>. So shall it be with man, the image of God. For the presents of God shall be seen on man and in him. On him because in the day that God shall reveal Himself in the brightness of His coming, He shall cloth man with Himself. And man shall appear as God outwardly. And in him because God has made His Temple to dwell in so that His Everlasting Works should be found there. And if man is seen doing good for <u>one</u> <u>another</u> and <u>seeking</u> to <u>preserve</u> the <u>creation</u>. Has not God already began inwardly to perform His Words? Indeed so, therefore God shall be seen in man and on him and man shall be as God, but not Him. Yea, the image but not the very thing. For God is Spirit and shall remain so because that which He <u>was</u>; He <u>is</u> and <u>shall</u> <u>be</u> for Ever and Ever .

Amen...

Knowing this we can then begin to understand the mystery of the Creation of God. Not God Creator, but rather God Head. This is to say, that which God Creator has set over His Creation. Even as it was in the Beginning of Days when the Shinning One was set over the Creation, even the First Estate. Nevertheless, the First Estate did fall and all that was left was found in the Garden of Eden. And it was called the Tree of the knowledge of good and evil. For it was God Himself that planted the Garden <u>eastward</u> in Eden. Nevertheless, the serpent was found as the keeper of this tree. For this was all that was left of the First Estate because when God's Spirit Visited the Creation of the <u>First Estate</u> He saw <u>Darkness</u> over the <u>face </u>of the <u>deep</u>. And the <u>Earth</u> was <u>without form</u> and <u>void</u>. Howbeit that in the Beginning God created the heaven and the earth and yet find the earth void and without form? Does the God of the Creation create in void or make things that have no form? For in the Beginning God Created

49

the _Heaven_ and the _Earth_. This was the First Estate for which Lucifer was the Shinning One, even the Cherub which covered (meaning from the beginning to the end). And as God said concerning him: he was found perfect in wisdom and beauty. In wisdom because he gave this light even as it was given him. In beauty because it was the Light of God. Nevertheless, the time came that this Great One saw that he was a likeness unto God, but not the image. And could not understand the purpose or the intent God had concerning this Work which He had done. For the image was yet forthcoming. The understanding was this: You can not please God without Faith. Yea, it was required of Lucifer to have faith concerning this Work which was to come. Even as the Lord spoke in His generation: to whom much is given, much is required. Yet Lucifer could not bear it. For it troubled him Greatly. For he desired to have knowledge of these things because he could not rest in Faith only. To this cause his wisdom became corrupt by reason of his brightness and in that day was iniquity found in his heart. From that time even until God visited His Creation, Lucifer began to hide this Light which was given him of God. That is to say concerning the image of God. For as the Lord said, Light is given not to be hidden, but to be put where all might see it. Now because Lucifer began to hide this Light a Darkness began to grow in the Heaven. And to this cause did the Earth become Void and without Form. For Lucifer desired to prevent God from making man an _image_ and likeness of Himself. For vanity took the place of Faith in Lucifer and he failed to understand God's wonderful and unlimited Power and the Works which He alone can do. For had Lucifer known he would not have feared the Works of God, but rather witnessed the Glory and the Righteousness of God. Nevertheless, the time came that God visited His Creation for the second time. Please understand the interpretation given here in. God meaning His very Spirit and not the God Head which was and is always with Him. As it is written of in Revelation. For John was _in_ Heaven when he saw the New Jerusalem _lowered down_ from _God_, even unto Heaven. For the Lord Himself said unto His people; before the foundation of the world, I am. And also this, as He prayed unto the Father saying; Glorify me with thyself as it was before the world began. This saying that God Head is that which God sets over the Kingdom, but is not the totality of God or He Himself. Even as Lucifer was set over the Kingdom in the Beginning of Days. Therefore understand this meaning of God visiting His Creation for the second time. For the first time was in the Creating itself and the second time was in the regeneration. And the final time shall be in the brightness of His coming. Even the Great White Throne Judgment. When Heaven and Earth shall flee from His Face and there was no place found for them. Once again I must say concerning this visitation of God, that I speak not of God Head, but rather God Almighty. For which God Head is with Him in this final visit. It was God Head that came in the Lord's coming and in the Millennium and also will be in the Rapture. This Kingdom or physical universe came into being through Lucifer. Not by him, but through him and to this cause did the Lord give us a parable concerning Himself. That He had to go to a far away place to receive His Kingdom. And also why He said unto Pilate; my Kingdom is not of this world. Let this not trouble you, but rather give you assurance that He the Lord comes to receive you unto Himself. And His Kingdom which shall surely come, for presently it is in

God Himself, but it shall surely manifest, even as this Kingdom <u>was</u> and <u>is</u>, but as it is written in the Word of God: it shall end with a Great noise and a fervent Heat and the elements shall melt and become a lake of fire which shall burn for ever and ever. For Gods judgment is Great, even as His Power. There are those who say this Kingdom will not end, but rather it will be perfected. This is not so, even by the words of our Lord. For if what they say is true. Why then does the Lord say He goes to prepare a place for us? Let not the sayings of the world deceive you, because this Kingdom or world has been cursed, even as Satan is cursed. To this cause was Satan cast unto the earth and sea. Does a wise man allow he who wishes to kill him to live in his house or does he cast him out? Therefore know and understand why the Lord returns not to setup a Kingdom, but rather to receive us and remove us from this place which is cast into the oven and also why He said flesh and blood can not enter into the Kingdom to come. Therefore have no fear as to what you shall eat or wear or even death itself. For it shall only be the flesh which passes away, but life shall continue. And if you fear not any of these things. How then shall the world deceive you? For it is by reason of fear of these things or should I say fear of losing these things that one is deceived. For God gave us life, even as He preserves it. For He is the provider and if you should hunger today He then shall feed you tomorrow. Likewise of all things of life. Even so oh Glorious One. For surely you come quickly.

Amen and Amen.......

Nevertheless, Lucifer changed this Light that was given him and said in his heart that he was doing even as God had done and therefore was equal to Him. And being equal to Him would not serve Him, but rather demand of Him. Even as it is written: this Evil One <u>believes</u> he has <u>changed</u> <u>times</u> and <u>laws</u>, but this is only the strong delusion God has given him because of his deceitfulness. For this one is truly the Father of Lies. Howbeit, that in the Garden of Eden this one did say unto Eve: <u>you shall not surely die</u> if you eat of this fruit. For God knows that the day you eat of it your eyes shall be opened and you shall be <u>as</u> <u>Gods</u>! And also this; And the Lord God said; behold, the man <u>is</u> <u>become</u> <u>as</u> <u>one</u> <u>of</u> <u>us</u>, to know good and evil: and now, least he put forth his hand and take also of the tree of life and eat and live for ever. Again I say, Howbeit that this Evil One is called the Father of Lies? And now I give you a mystery. This One became the Father of Lies long before the Day of Adam and Eve. That which he spoke to Eve was not a lie by reason of the words, but rather by reason of the intent of his heart. Because the words of the Lord God were the same, but not the intent. Nevertheless, it was in the First Estate that this One became the Father of Lies, because he took the Light given him and did change it. To this cause did the Spirit of God move upon the face of the waters when there was darkness upon the face of the deep in the night of the beginning of Days concerning the Son of the Morning. Even the First Estate. For in the Beginning God Created the Heaven and the Earth: Yet the Earth was found without form and void, because the Evil One did change the Light of God and to this cause he became the Father of Lies. And this is the reason that this Evil One changed the Light of God. The Son of the Morning was a likeness unto God, but not the image; Yet he was also a Son of God and to this

51

cause he came to know Great things, nevertheless with knowledge comes sorrows and without Faith sorrows become corruption and this Great One could not rest in Faith alone; Yet you can not please God without Faith. To this cause the Light given to this Great One was not allowed to be seen. And this Light was the coming of the image of God, even Adam. Therefore God Himself, that is to say God the Creator and His Christ (God Head) said let us make man in our image after our likeness. Indeed, He Himself brought this work and manifestation into being. Because it was seen not in the First Estate as it was given to him, the Evil One. To this cause was Adam made complete (Image of God), even as God is complete and not as the beast of the fields, both male and female. And all was brought before Adam, as God was with him. Then in the passing of days, after all things were brought before Adam. He was then made both male and female and their name was called Adam. Yea, it was in that day that Adam, that is to say Eve fell into transgression and Satan gained authority over them (Adam) because of his deceitfulness. The reason why he gained authority over them is because they as a whole came out of the earth, yet they lived not by the earth, but by God and the trees which He planted for them. To be as meat. But they being driven out of the Garden they had to live by the earth which belongs unto Satan. And to this cause was the tree of the knowledge of good and evil found in the mist of the garden. And the serpent was the keeper thereof. And because they did eat of this tree they must then live by it and its keeper which has been made to eat from the dust of the ground. And God did curse the ground for Adam's sake. Know this concerning the Evil One. Where he is, so is his Kingdom (Woe unto the earth and the sea because the Devil is cast down unto you). Where is the seed of the serpent and who are the children of Eve? The latter is easy for us to answer because the Lord came unto mankind, even the Lord of Glory. As it was promised to Eve and her seed in the beginning of days. Yet, the former came before mankind and we remember him not. And this One who comes in his own name. Will he call us his children? For even though he has remained unseen, he has influenced all of us with his knowledge and ways. And has he not entered into the temple of God and shows himself as God in the day that he is seen? Oh children of the resurrection, this One shall know you even if you remember him not! Yea, many do honor him for he is their God, even as he is their knowledge and strength, which they do trust in. For truly, truly they shall behold the beast and wonder whose names are not written in the book of life. Because they trust in the knowledge of the world and not the knowledge of God, which is His Word and His Promise which He gave to us first by reason of the law and the prophets. And then came the Lord Himself to reveal the things that come here after. And that we must trust in Him and His Works and not the knowledge the Evil One gives us that we should be deceived by him and to worship him by reason of his strength. For if we trust in our knowledge of this Kingdom, then we are living by the Evil One and we are giving him the glory. Therefore he becomes our God. But if we trust in the Lord and His works and wait on His promises to be fulfilled. Then we are living by Him who is alive and even though we use the knowledge of this world that we are in. We are not living by it, but by the spirit of the Lord. For He has become the Tree of Life by which we live. And we are found without the mark of the beast on our hand or on our forehead. We will not be seen doing the works of Satan by the works of our hands. Nor the will of Satan by the desires of our heart. Because we seek the will of our Lord and wait for His guidance concerning the things that we do. And it is our Faith in Him that keeps us. Even so Oh Lord.

Amen and Amen.......

And these are the things concerning Son of God, even He who was given all authority, all power and all judgment over mankind. Because He is Son of Man. Yea, He entered man and became a likeness unto him. Even as He is a perfect image of God. To this cause was He created before the foundation of the earth and became the beginning of the creation of God. For if God Almighty had a beginning He would be as such a Child as The Son of God, even The Only Begotten. Nevertheless, His power and His authority is given of the Most High. He who is the "Only", even the Great I Am. That His will should be done. And His will is that His likeness and image should not perish but have everlasting life Inherent. Therefore, Son of Man draws all men unto Him, those with some understanding and others with no understanding. That is to say, those alive in Christ and also those dead in Christ. For each have a part and must fulfill it. Howbeit that a man can be in Christ and yet be dead? By reason of that which entered there in. For Christ entered into that which became dead when man fell from God in the beginning of days. Even so, by Christ entering into that which was dead (man) there was then found life in what had become dead. And though he was dead, yet shall he live by Christ Jesus. Yes, there are those who say that if a man dies while believing in Christ Jesus, he then is dead in Christ. And this is true, and I say unto you if a man is found in Christ though he may appear dead outwardly he is very much alive inwardly. And he is only sleeping because he only taste death. For the Lord Himself said such an one is passed from death unto life. Indeed, if a man is in Christ, he is in that which is alive and there is no death in Him. Again, as the Lord said; God is not the God of the dead, but of the living. Truly, truly that which is found in Christ is alive and that which Christ enters and remains is resurrected unto life. For the Lord God of Host searches the hearts of men that they might receive Him or reject Him. For judgment was given unto Him and to this cause did He Himself say; God judges no man, but has given judgment to son of man and He shall judge much concerning man. For He is the Lord of the Sabbath and Almighty God, even the Spirit of Truth has found rest in Him concerning man who is made in the image and likeness of God.

Amen.......

Lucifer, Lucifer how art thou fallen oh Lucifer Son of the Morning : Know then the meaning of this saying and how we should interpret its meaning? It is also written: Iniquity was found in his heart. Consider this in your heart and hear with understanding: This Lucifer, the Shinning One who was perfect in wisdom and beauty who became that which, was, and is not, and yet is: How was iniquity found in his heart if he was perfect in beauty and wisdom? Indeed he was perfect in wisdom and beauty, but not in Faith, because he was the Accuser

53

of the brethren (man) and could not walk in <u>Faith</u> of God's Mystery concerning the <u>Image</u> of <u>God</u>, that is to say Man. To this cause did he become the Accuser of the brethren, for he desired for God <u>not</u> to have an image, yet desired to be equal to God. He not knowing that he was already as God, yet to be perfected in Faith of God or rather a God like Faith. It is written that it is impossible to please God without <u>Faith</u> . And that God has taken the simple (Faith) to lay a way for Salvation and has made it a stumbling block for the wise and prudent. For so it seems good in His sight that He gave this Truth to Babes (little Ones) and they perfected Praise unto the Lord. For the same are <u>they</u> the <u>host</u> that Lucifer "Himself" cast down from Heaven while he was yet in Heaven. This is to say the host that were trodden under foot for a time and times and the dividing of times. And among them was one as Mary, the Blessed Mother of God. And the second Adam came as Son of Man (Son of God) through the name (parable) of Jesus ; meaning Joshua as God had promised in him. And Mary Blessed Mother of the Church. To whom God fulfilled His Word (Promise) to Glorify woman. That He turned away from her for awhile, but that He would Glorify her in due season. For as it was in the beginning so shall it be in its end, that is to say perfect in its generation. It shall fulfill its purpose. For Mary indeed is the Mother of God, for Jesus was raised up by God the Father unto His Throne and has received All Authority and All Power and All Judgment, even unto the Father. For All Things must be put Under Him and Subjected to Him. Therefore <u>He</u> <u>is</u> <u>God</u>!!! Glory be to the Lord of Lords and King of Kings, even so Father

Amen.......

Now if Jesus is God than Mary His Mother is chosen of God. I tell you a Truth, Jesus is Son of Man and Son of Man is spirit and spirit God is, was, and will be. For No Man is God, yet man is an image of God. Yea, the flesh profits nothing and it was not the flesh of Jesus, but rather the Spirit and Soul of Jesus that has saved us. He denied the flesh and gave it for our Salvation. To this cause understand this saying of Jesus "man" who came though this Host that was cast down by Lucifer. Even Mary His Mother. Which gave birth to the flesh, even as God gave birth to His Spirit. This does not make them Less Holy before God. For it was the Holy Spirit that remembered Mary and it was the seed in her that made the flesh of Jesus. But it was the Holy Spirit that Sanctified the Spirit of Jesus and made Him a Most Holy Living Soul. Our Lord is perfect in Faith of God, and in Lucifer was No Faith found. Only perfect in Wisdom and Beauty. To say perfect in wisdom and beauty is referring to the perfection of Life on All levels of being, both physical and spirit. And its progression and ability to limit itself each to it's time and season. That is to say if you should supply water to a portion of the dry desert it would in time become an oasis and life would appear and progress. This being true to All forms of life in All worlds that could support its forms of Life, whether it be small or whether it be great. Consider this which you call "Mother Nature" and how different forms of life are Natural enemies, to say weighed one against the other to keep the balance to the time and season (which some call "evolution"). And when a given form of life becomes extinct, then its season has past. Yet like the desert if another time and season should come so also would *that form of life return. Know then that there is One who has put His Power in the times and seasons. It is in this Power that you have Life and also Death. And He requires you to walk in His Faith, which is your believing in His Son, which is Jesus Christ, and if you believe then you shall find a desire in you to be like minded in this manner; to be forgiving one to the other, even if it takes a little time continue to seek and it is found. To love one another, which is to give even as it is given unto you. What is your Ability? What things have you been able to learn? The same is that which you have been given. He to whom much is given, much is required. And likewise, he to whom little is given, little is required. To this cause is it said from our Lord Jesus Christ; Blessed are the poor for theirs is the Kingdom of God. This saying is not for those who have received much for they have their part, but rather for those who are born (baptized) into sorrows; for to Glorify God; to say manifestation of God. Now as to he to whom much is given, whether it be knowledge, whether it be wealth, whether it be skill for All are gifts. If he should give alms of those things which he has, share or help others with that which he has rather than storing up things Only for himself, then behold All things are made clean unto him. As to He who is the times and seasons, it is He for whom All things were and are created, which is for His pleasure. This meaning that the Only <u>death</u> is by reason of His displeasure. For He shall not Remember them in Life, Resurrection of Righteousness but rather in <u>death</u>, Resurrection of damnation. And each shall remain in their place which is in God the Father of Creation, who has put His Great Power in the times and seasons. For the things that were and are created came out of God in its time and season, then consumed or returned unto Him. For He is a consuming God. Yet, there is a time promised of Him, that He shall walk openly in an Everlasting Creation and Man shall be His Image. Hallelujah His "True" Image, so that God and Man shall walk as One forever and ever, even so Father.*

Amen and Amen.......

Now in the Everlasting Creation, Resurrection of Righteousness, there is no place found for death, sorrow, to say all of these is only to say damnation (hell). For God has promised to not Remember sin in this Everlasting Kingdom whose dominion is forever even for ever and ever. Yet there is a Resurrection of damnation, even as it was spoken of by our Lord Jesus Christ and this Resurrection of damnation shall burn forever, even forever and ever and God shall put a Great Gulf Fixed between the Everlasting Kingdom and the Lake of Fire and "None" shall pass thru Him (The Lord of Lords and King of Kings). And then shall the Sons of God Shine and bring forth Light and be Stars of The Everlasting Kingdom. For God shall enter into the temple and shall open The Ark of His Testimony and Reveal unto His Creation the Great Riches of His Glory (Joy, Peace, Love, to say All Righteousness), His Perfection. Now in the Recreation there shall be many Levels, even as this Kingdom has many Levels. For this Kingdom is but shadows of things to come. Which is to say, the good and beautiful things seen and heard are images of things that are and will be (The Everlasting Kingdom). And of these many Levels of the "New Kingdom" there are the Small and Great Ones. They who dwell on High (Great Ones), the same are Strong and Remember the place of damnation.

And to this cause they are with Him to whom All things are Subjected to and put under, Our Lord Jesus Christ, "The Great Gulf Fixed". And concerning the Small Ones, the same are they who know not sorrow, nor pain, nor death, who have become the Images of Beauty, Love, Joy. To use an old saying; Heaven on Earth a Recreated Earth; One with <u>No Sea</u>; your body dies not to say your worm dies and you know not death. To put it another way so that those dull of hearing might see. Our body (matter) as in this Kingdom has a so called Life Cycle and its structure (Electrical charge of particles) begins to neutralize and break down to ionized particles and neutrons. Which is only to say this Kingdom's days are numbered whether they are wise enough to see it or not. For our Lord Christ said that God would not give the True Riches unto those whose names were not written in the Book of Life. And the Book of Life is not on the Earth, neither is it under the Earth, but rather in Heaven and likewise the True Riches. Therefore know that the True Riches are not of this Kingdom. This Kingdom must pass away so that The Everlasting Kingdom might take on form, Everlasting form. Therefore the Great Ones shall serve God by reason of His Greatness and the Small Ones shall Glorify Him by reason of His Glory. This meaning that those on High shall remember of sin that it shall remain in its place outside of the Everlasting Kingdom (Utter Darkness). So that the Lake of Fire should burn and its smoke ascend up unto God forever and ever. And that the Small Ones, the same shall God walk one with and with them (Small Ones) He should Not Remember Sin. For these Small Ones shall know Not Sin. Only God's Glory shall their Light be. For these things which I speak the same did Jesus speak to the disciples when He said: I have yet many things to say unto you, but you cannot bear them now. Which is also why He said unto them (disciples) to stay away from controversial matters for it breaks Unity, to say it brings offenses and if you find offenses, how will you find the Spirit of Truth for He is of Single eye and speaks not His Own, but that which He hears. This being Unity for God is complete and has No needs and that which He gives fulfills All Needs that are Created. Yea, God made His Works and they are Non ending. To this cause has He chosen to save a portion of man (Son of Man and All that are in Him). And take man into eternity with Him. This being the Everlasting Kingdom. For there is No Need for any of the Little Ones to prove the Truth which he might speak, for Christ Jesus has Already overcome the world and it is sufficient for God because He has Glorified it and even Now is He Glorifying it again. This being so because as the Son came in the form of a man Glorified by the Holy Spirit, so also must the Father likewise. This is only to say His Spirit enters into a man (temple). Which is made spirit of itself by reason of the creation. To say, He (Father) enters into the Creation. His by the Power of God the Father of Creation (Creator). For the Father and the Son are the God Head and the Holy Spirit the Power and the Authority (Creators Blessing unto Adam) over All the Creation. To say He who sits upon the Throne is to say Father. And the Spirit of Truth, even the Holy Spirit proceeds forth from the Father (He who sits upon the throne). Now the Father and the Son are one. The Son in the Father and the Father in the Son. The meaning is this; As the Father has Life in Himself so also the Son of Man has Life in Himself. This being the commandment given unto the Son by the Father, which is only to say through the Holy Spirit that came down from God the (Creator) unto Adam. Now this saying of <u>Life in Himself</u> speaks of the Holy Spirit which God Himself (Creator) "breathed" into Adam in the beginning of Life unto the image of God. To this cause the Father and the Son have <u>Life in Himself</u> and in this Oneness shall the Sons of God (Little Ones) be baptized with the Holy Spirit so that they might become One, even as the Father and the Son are One. For it is the Spirit that Quickens, even the Spirit of Truth. And He shall move when He will, which is the season given Him and the time appointed even in the beginning when All and All was One. For the time comes and is come that All the Sons of God's Righteousness shall be One, even as the Father and the Son are One. By reason of the Holy Spirit, which is God's Blessing come down unto His Creation. Even so Father

Amen........

Yea, the Sons of God (Little Ones) are in the Son (the Only Begotten of God, that is to say the Only One He should Glorify before men and Angels by reason of the Works given Him and fulfilled by Him). Again I say, the Little Ones are in the Son and are made One, even as the Son is in the Father and they are One. As it is written in Revelation 3:21; To him that over cometh will I grant to sit with Me in My throne, even as I also overcame and am set down with My Father in His throne. To say with Him is to say two (2) Spirits yet One Soul (Holy Spirit, Blessing come down from God {Creator} unto Adam) To this cause are they One. For it is the Holy Spirit, even the Spirit of Truth which said: I Am the First and the Last the Alpha and Omega. And by this Truth are the Father and the Son made One. Consider also as it is written in Revelation 3:14; These things saith the Amen, the Faithful and True Witness, <u>the beginning of the Creation of God</u>: This meaning that through the coming of the Son the Mystery of the Creation of God began before men. What God is this speaking of ? Why it's the Godhead (Father, Son, Holy Spirit)!.. Why then does it begin with the Son and not the Father ? Because the Father died that the Son might come. And by the Son coming the Father can be put under Him, that is to say <u>all</u> <u>things</u> are <u>given Him</u>. And by what Power was the Son Raised up ? By the Power of God (Creator) who raised Him up even unto the Throne by reason of the Holy Spirit (Blessing come down from God {Creator} unto Adam). To this cause is Adam raised up in the Last Days that the Kingdom of God might be delivered up, even the Father. Yet, if the Father died that the Son might come; who sat on the throne in His coming ? The Holy Spirit is He who Lives forever and ever and He who sat upon the throne even as the Son was caught up unto the throne. To this cause did Jesus say that He must leave the world so that the Comforter (Holy Spirit) might come and Reprove the world of sin, and of Righteousness and of Judgment. That is to say, the Holy Spirit shall baptize the Sons of God that they might be One in the Father even as Our Lord Christ Jesus said as He prayed unto the Father in John 17:20-23. Therefore know and understand who dwells with us in these Days. For No <u>Man</u> knowth the <u>Son, but</u> the <u>Father</u> and likewise, No <u>Man</u> knowth the <u>Father, but</u> the <u>Son</u> and He to whom He reveals it unto. This saying that both the Father and the Son must come in the form of a man. Let me explain: It is written and said by our

Lord Jesus Christ that No _Man but_ the Son or No _Man but_ the Father. This saying that there are a few men who would know and also that the Father and the Son should come as Man and therefore be raised up among men. Yet it is said that Adam fell from God (Creator) and was cursed and forsaken. He was _not_ cursed by God. He was told that He would _surly die_. For the Son is a Perfect Image of the Father and had to die and be raised up unto God (First Resurrection). And therefore likewise has the Father tasted death in the beginning of days (first) and therefore in the Last Days shall be raised up unto God (Second Resurrection). So Adam fell from God, but not his soul (breath of Life). It was Adam's Spirit that fell and not his soul. Let me explain: First let us consider Christ Jesus. He being the Son of the Godhead came (sent, not fallen) unto this Kingdom and as He was being crucified He said; Father, I commend My Spirit into Your Hands. This meaning that only His Spirit had entered into this Kingdom. Even as He said; the only thing that can ascend into Heaven is that which descended down from Heaven. With this Truth consider also Hebrews 4:12; For the _Word_ of _God_ is _Quick_, and _Powerful_, and _Sharper_ than _Any_ _two-edged_ _sword_, _piercing_ even to the _dividing_ _Asunder_ of _Soul_ and _Spirit_, and of the joints and marrow, and is a discerner of the thoughts and intents of the heart. This showing that God (Creator) has divided the Soul and Spirit of some (the host which Satan cast out of Heaven, which God allowed him to do even as he was allowed to test Job). And the same host became Just Men, but not Perfect. For Christ Jesus had not yet come while they were cast down. And in His coming they were made perfect by reason of Faith in the Son of God, Christ Jesus. Consider again Hebrews 12:22-24; But ye have come unto Mount Sion, and unto the city of the Living God, the Heavenly Jerusalem, and to an innumerable company of Angels. To the general assembly and _Church_ of the _firstborn_, which are _written_ _in_ _Heaven_ and to God the Judge of All, and to the _Spirits_ of _Just_ _men_ _made_ _perfect_. And to _Jesus_ the _Mediator_ of the _New Covenant_, and to the blood of Sprinkling, that _speaketh_ _better_ _things_ _than_ _that_ _of_ _Abel_. Therefore know that Christ Jesus was sent unto us by the Father that we might know Him. And by knowing Him we shall also know of His Chastening. For if we endure His Chastening, God then deals with us as with His Sons; for what son is he whom the father chastens not ? Consider again Hebrews 12:9; Furthermore we have had fathers of our flesh which corrected us, and we gave them reverence: shall we not much rather be in subjection unto the Father of Spirits, and Live ? Yet, who is the Father of Spirits ? Consider this: All men came forth from Adam the Father of All flesh. To this cause are All men born in death. Nevertheless, God blessed Adam and to this cause came the First Fruits. That is to say the church of the Firstborn, who are the Righteous. This meaning just men made perfect by the coming of Jesus (Son of Man). To also say the heritage of Seth, which is again the blessing come down from God (Creator) unto Adam. Now if Adam is cursed and not forgiven; Howbeit, his son who is of him can receive the blessing of the righteous? Can unrighteousness beget righteousness ? God forbid ! The answer is this: God has not cursed Adam, but rather cursed the ground for Adam's sake. Nor has God forsaken Adam, because the Sons of Righteousness came through him, this is to say the Church of the First-born (House of God). To this cause do I tell you that Adam is blessed and not cursed and *that his fall was not a fall unto destruction but rather a fall unto a Holy Mountain, because he was truly blessed of God and God's works can not fail Him. And also this; the seed of Seth (good) and the seed of Cain (forsaken and cursed) both came out of Adam and to this cause is he the Father of spirits. Not the Father of Creation, but rather the Father of Godhead because God Himself (Creator) breathed life into Adam and it is not possible that God should error or His works should fail Him. So Adam became the Father of All flesh, and because he is blessed and not cursed he also was given the throne and became the Father of Spirits, that is to say the Father of Godhead. This is so because in the beginning God blessed Adam and gave him dominion over every living thing that moveth upon the earth. As it is written in Genesis 2:19; And out of the ground the Lord God formed every beast of the field, and every fowl of the air; and brought them unto Adam to see what he would call them: And whatsoever Adam called every <u>living creature</u>, that was the name thereof. And Adam gave names to All cattle, and to the fowl of the air, and to every beast of the field; This showing the Authority given Adam by God the Father of Creation. For God brought All Living Creatures unto Adam, meaning that he sat upon a throne and named them. Please understand, Adam as flesh did not sit upon a throne, but rather his soul and spirit sat upon the throne and in his falling was his spirit and soul divided asunder and his spirit fell unto a Holy Mountain, and it was upon this Holy Mountain that the Church of the Firstborn came forth, even the House of God. This being shown by Moses the servant of God when he restored unto the children of God that which is written in the Book of Genesis concerning the Creation and the sons of Adam. Let me begin in this manner; If you will notice the names of Adam's sons form a given pattern. That is to say; the names of the firstborn is given and the rest of Adam's children are spoken of as sons and daughters. This stands true for All of the firstborn from Seth even to Noah. The only exception is in the very beginning when Cain and Abel are born. Cain of course being the First born and Abel the Last. Now it was at this point that Adam raised his sons and taught them of God and how they should Please Him, that is to say ; Love the Lord God with All of your heart and All of your soul and with All of your might. And also to honour your Father and Mother and to love one another, even as God loves you. Then in the passing of time they became old enough to bring before the Lord God an offering of their labour, even as it was instructed unto them, each their own part, for each is needed. And as they gave their offerings unto the Lord God, His Holy Spirit spoke unto them. And unto the Last born Abel, the Lord God said "The First shall be Last and the Last shall be First". And the Lord God found Respect unto Abel and his offering. And then unto the Firstborn, Cain, the Lord God said "Because you are the first, even as your Father before you, so shall you also be last. For the God of Heaven and Earth has chosen to Judge "Himself". Therefore shall the House of God be divided and Judged first. Then shall man the image of God be Judged of himself, for he is truly an image of God and thereby a likeness unto Him. Then Cain's countenance fell and he became envious of his younger brother, and the Holy Spirit said unto Cain the elder and firstborn, why art thou wroth ? And why is thy countenance fallen ? If thou doest well (be patient), shall thou not be accepted (that is to say, have the excellency)?*

And if thou doest not well, sin lieth at the door. And unto thee shall be his desire (that is to say, and the way of sin shall you feel a need of and it will seem right unto you), and thou shall rule over him. This meaning that in a time which shall come unto Cain he shall be delivered from this sin and shall rule over its ways. To this cause did Cain go unto his brother Abel and talked with him. Because the Holy Spirit of God did come unto him to comfort him concerning his younger brother and the words (spirit) that came down from God. This restoring Cain's countenance even to a passing of time when in the field with his brother Abel, the sin that was at the door Rose up in him and likewise did Cain against Abel his brother and did slay him with his hand. Now God had respect for Abel and his offering and to this cause Abel's Life or Blood was one with God and when he was slain God heard the voice of his blood or Life Cry unto Him even as he saw the Earth open Her Mouth to receive his blood or Life from him. To this cause was Cain cursed from the face of the Earth. Because the Earth had received the blood of the first of the Sons of Righteousness by his hand. And he would not find Rest in the Earth, but rather to be a Vagabond and a fugitive for the Earth would not receive his blood or Life even until the Last Days. This being so because after God spoke to Cain concerning his punishment, Cain said unto the Lord, Mine iniquity is greater than that it may be forgiven. Behold, thou hast driven me out this day from the face of the Earth; and from thy face shall I be hid. This meaning he would not be able to find rest or peace in the Lord or in the Earth. That death shall flee from him, that is to say death would not keep him. To this cause did God put a mark upon Cain. And the Lord said unto him, Therefore, whosoever slayeth Cain, Vengeance shall be taken on him sevenfold. And the Lord set a mark upon Cain, least any finding him should Kill him. This saying that God did not want anyone Killing Cain except those who were worthy of vengeance. And should they kill him the Earth would then receive the blood of the sevenfold (those worthy of vengeance) rather then receive Cain's blood. For that which God hides, only He can reveal and also this; by God's words Cain can not die, be killed, only hurt. Even until the End of Days. For that which was first the Lord has made last and the last shall be first. For God has saved the seed of Cain for the Last Days, that is to say, He the Lord shall Redeem a portion of the seed of Cain and the Father shall enter into flesh under the Name of Cain. For the Son came under the Name of Abel, to this cause was His Life shortened or cut off and also why he had no children of the flesh and was found perfect before God. This also being the reason why Jesus said there be eunuchs, which have made themselves eunuchs for the Kingdom of Heaven's sakes. That is to say to remain untouched as a virgin. And to eat of the things of God only rather then the things of men. This meaning to be sent to this Kingdom and not fallen. He to whom it is given surely he shall receive it. This being a manifestation of God to fulfill God's words, because few receive this saying, yet many are saved because the few came not to be saved, but to save as many as would Receive He who sent them, even the Son of God, Christ Jesus and the Holy Father.

Amen.......

To this cause did Jesus say; he who Receives Me Receives He who sent Me. Therefore know and understand the parable of Cain and Abel. For the Son of Man has indeed come under the Name of Abel and His Life among men is a testimony unto this truth, that is also to say a likeness unto it. And again also do I tell you that the Father of Man has come under the Name of Cain and his life or parable is a likeness unto him. To this cause has the Names of Cain and Abel been separated from All the other Sons of Adam from Seth even unto Noah. <u>Because</u> of <u>the Father</u> and <u>the Son</u> which <u>were yet to come when Moses</u> did <u>write about them</u>. Now from Seth to Noah was the pattern set, that is to say the name of the firstborn was given and the rest of the children were called sons and daughters. The names of the Firstborn from Seth unto Noah are only nine. Yet the House of God has been given to be ten (10), even as Moses has said and as God has shown by reason of Pharaoh in the day that God delivered His chosen people from Egypt and <u>hardened Pharaoh's heart</u> so that the plagues would number ten (10), which is to say God would show His Works ten (10) times before the house of Pharaoh so that All might know that it indeed was God Revealing the Power of the House of God unto All the Earth, far and near, even to this day. Nevertheless, the number of Names written in the Book of Life which was given unto the Lamb is ten (10). Now Seth is not the first name, but the second which was written, for the First Name is Abel, yet there are better things spoken of then that of Abel. For the First shall be Last and the Last shall be First. And also this, the Lord Christ Jesus did the Works given Him of the Father and then He said: Greater Works then these shall you do. This speaking of the Last Days when the Evil One should be Revealed and his Hour of Greatness should come and How if it were possible he should deceive the very Elect (the remnant of her seed). To this cause do the Greater Works come in the Last Days when this Evil One exalts himself before the two (2) witnesses and they who are able to hear their testimony, for it is the Father's Works that is Greater than All and He Himself should come in the Days of the Greater Works or how else could it come for when God created All things He Himself, Gave the Son His Works in the Morning and the Father His Works in the Evening so that each should have a part, that is to say, the First shall be Last and the Last shall be First. This also meaning the beginning of the Creation of God coming to an end (Godhead complete, Father being subjected unto the Son) and the Everlasting Creation coming to its beginning of transformation. That is to say, Brightness of His Coming or Recreation.. For the Mystery of the Creation of God had its beginning therefore it <u>must</u> have an end, yet it is everlasting. What then is the understanding? When the end of this Kingdom is fully come the Kingdom of God (New Heaven and Earth) shall enter into the Eternal, that is to say, be transformed and become Non ending. To this cause is it written in Revelation that when the White Throne Judgment is come there will be no place found for Heaven and Earth. For this Universe (Kingdom) is, but an image of things that Are, yet not a true image, and in this time which is come, the true Image of the Eternal shall become visible (Brightness of His Coming) and to this cause shall the Everlasting Kingdom be as the Eternal, that is to say No beginning, Nor No End, because it has always been with Him, even before the beginning, when the foundation of the Earth was found. Even so Father.

Amen and Amen....

Now as it was said the Lambs Book of Life has ten (10) Names written and under each of these Names are one thousand (1,000) Names, these being the Ten Thousand spoken of by Enoch and also the number mentioned in Isaiah 60:22; A Little One shall become a thousand, and a small One a Strong Nation. I the lord will hasten it in his time. The ten thousand as Enoch said would come with the Lord, that is to say the First Resurrection and the Small One or Great Nation would come in the Second Resurrection. The understanding is this: From Abraham came the twelve tribes of Israel and also from Abraham by reason of Ishmael came a portion of the twelve tribes of the World and their nations. Now in them are some that are just and some that are evil. To this cause in the Second Resurrection they that were Lost in evil would be gathered unto One Nation, for they are children of Abraham. Not All, but yet part and God Loves His friend. Even as the Lord Loved and called the disciples (Elect) His friends. And forgets them not and to this cause are they (the small ones) gathered unto One Nation which would be Great for God is kind to these small ones and has taken many kindreds and tongues and made them one people and they are Great upon the face of the earth. And they are a testimony unto the world that the Lord has done this thing for it was He Himself that said; Blessed are the peace makers for they shall be called the children of God. And in this day is it known that this Great Nation of many peoples is looked upon as the peacemakers of the world. Therefore know that this Great Nation and the people thereof have received this Blessing of plenty by reason of inheritance and not by merit and God's words are fulfilled and He has done it. For I tell you a Truth, Abraham is a friend of God because God chose him and took him apart from among men and made him to hear and to walk before Him and to believe and wait for His counsel. To this cause did Abraham say; shall the Lord speak and Abraham not hear. Nevertheless, this offspring of Abraham by which the Small Ones came was the firstborn of Abraham thereby being the last to receive God's Grace. And it is by this Truth that I tell you that this thing which the Lord has done was and is for the Second Resurrection. And to this do I say he who has an ear to hear, let him hear and understand; the small ones have become Strong Nations, yet if they will not take heed to what the Spirit speaks unto the Nations, even that which he has shall be taken away and given unto he who is most fruitful, which shall bring this Glory given even unto Heaven. Therefore, let every strong Nation that stands in this present generation know that their works do follow them and that the God of All and All is in secret and sees All works done and as He sees them doing so also does He give unto them, for the workmen is worthy of his hire. Now as to the First Resurrection I must mention again the Book of Life and the ten (10) thousand Names written, for under these Names are found other names of which were one hundred fold, and from these came the one hundred forty and four thousand (144,000) and of the remainder are those who partake of the Second Resurrection as priests of God and His Christ and also those of the one thousand year millennium.. Let me explain, before Christ's coming in the time of the prophets there was manifested unto men the ten (10) thousand, which is the Lord who rose up early and sent the Law and the Prophets. For this number was found in Adam and they came from the ten (10) Names God chose by reason of the Firstborn and these being the Little Ones, which became the thousand. Now in Christ coming His Voice was heard of them and from the time of the Lord's Resurrection until the end time of John (he who tarried for the Lord) these Little Ones became an hundred fold which was their fruitfulness. Yea, it was at this time that the Lord came in silence and received unto Himself the Church of the Firstborn and the fruitfulness thereof, even the hundred fold and Heaven was closed and the Marriage of the Lamb took place. And the vials were poured out unto All the inhabitancy of the earth. To this cause No Man was able to witness or know of these things which took place because it was done before God in Heaven and therefore done in secret, because He is in Secret. Now there are those who say this marriage must take place on earth because the Angels are not given in Marriage. Consider this my friends; the Lord is Above the Angels and God has given unto Him what He has given to None other. And by this Truth when the Lord came among us He did what None other Man did. Nevertheless, this Great multitude or hundred fold (100) are those which partook of the Marriage Supper of the Lamb. And while this took place in Heaven the vials were being poured out upon the Earth. From the time the pouring out of the vials began to its end, the passing of days was approximately eight hundred (800) years. Then Heaven was opened and the twelve (12) Throne Judgment began and likewise the Millennium. For in the Millennium the Judgment is its Power and its Righteousness. And those who partook of the Millennium lived many Names each to his several ability and in this fruitfulness came the sixty (60) fold which are partaking of the Second Resurrection, even this day and among them are those who lived not again until the Millennium was (fulfilled), finished and also among this number are those who partook of the First Resurrection and entering in as priests of God and His Christ. And as to the hundred forty and four thousand (144,000), they remain with Christ and go withersoever He goeth. For in God's House are many (Mansions), dwelling places. It is so, because the Lord has told us this in His Words, that we might be assured that as there is a place in Him for us, so also is there a place in us for Him. Let us then Rejoice in this hour that is upon us for the Lord is prepared to receive us (Church, Remnant of her seed) unto Himself. The flesh is weak, but the spirit is indeed willing. For the Rapture is before us, even at the doors. But this is not the end, but rather the beginning of the Testimony of the two (2) witnesses and also the Great Tribulation upon the World. Yea, the earth shall be moved from her place in this day. And another shall come and his power is Great before men, but not before the two (2) witnesses for they know his name and their time of Power is come. For in the Rapture are they made Alive and Remain for a short time. And it is from their Testimony that the thirty fold (30) shall be received unto the Lord, even the stranger for whom the Lord has called into His presence. For in the beginning of days he was driven out of the presence of the Lord, even as Adam the man was driven out of the Garden of Eden. But in these Last Days he shall Remember from whence he has fallen and shall see the Works of the Lord and shall Glorify His Name. For he who is Last to Receive the Lord, the same was also first to hear Him. But also first to deny the Lord and to turn away. This was done to fulfill the Words of <u>God Almighty</u> in the beginning of days, when He gave His

Testimony of All things from the beginning, even to its end. For the time is coming and is come that the inhabitance of Heaven are able to see the Ark of His Testament (God Almighty), and shall also see that which is written thereon, and in that day shall <u>God Almighty</u> be seen standing Gloriously before His Ancients and the tribes of the Earth shall mourn. Know you not that the Creator is complete, which is only to say He Always was, is, and will be. Yet, it is said that He took apart of Himself and Created All Things. If He took a part of Himself; How then can He be whole ? By reason of His Laws of Creation, for which one is the Law of Giving. The same is it that keeps Him Whole. Give and it shall be given unto you, some thirty (30) fold, some sixty (60) fold, and some one hundred fold (100). Now when the Creator took of Himself (Gave), He then received even more then He Gave, yet if He is truly whole, then He needs not more unless He is not complete in Himself. For which He is. To this cause came the Mystery of the Creation of God (Godhead). Therefore the Creator remained whole and complete and that which was the increase became the Godhead.. For God is the increase. Now the Son became the perfect image of God and the Father a perfect Spirit or perfect will of God (Creator). This being so by reason of the Holy Spirit, which is the Power and Authority and Most of all the Unity of the Father and the Son. Which is the Blessing come down from God (Creator) unto His Creation. To this cause is the Holy Spirit, even the Spirit of Truth, Most Sacred and also the Father being as the Son. And the Son as the Father. Yet, they are One by reason of the Holy Spirit. And in this Oneness shall the Creator walk in His Creation, even as it was in the beginning, when He would come in the cool of the evening and walk in the Garden with Adam (in Adam). Even so Father. Amen and Amen... For God's Glory is made for God's Temple and God's Temple is Man. To this cause when God's Glory enters into man which is the image of God, then man becomes As God. To this cause man is and was created and recreated in Christ Our Lord. For He has become the Recreated Man (Adam), Image of God. As God, Lord of the Creation. The Recreation, Everlasting Kingdom and the Children of Light shall become the Sons of God and be As Him, forever and ever more.

Amen and Amen.......

The Son of God came not for the Righteous, but rather the unrighteous (Acts 10:34). Meaning those who have fallen, yet nevertheless those who were righteous were given Him (Christ Jesus) by God (Father) which are the First fruits. For this reason was it necessary for the Righteous to receive Christ Jesus as Lord. As was required by Cornelius in a vision to learn of Jesus Christ that He might believe on Him and be saved. Indeed, he was drawn unto the Lord. Where then did the fall come from? Was it not Adam who fell and therefore All are fallen ? The answer is given by Daniel, first know this; the first Adam as the second was required to die that He might be fruitful. As Jesus said: If a kernel of corn is put in the earth and dies it brings forth much fruit. To this cause did Adam fall and die and by this cause is Adam the Father of All flesh. Now the Son of Man (meaning the son of Adam, the second Adam) was and is the blessing of God the Father of Creation to the first Adam, He to come out of women <u>Eve</u>, (Son of Godhead). Now because Eve came out of Adam, it then became

64

necessary for the Son of Man, the second Adam, to come out of woman (Eve). For God promised to Glorify woman (Eve), and to this cause did God have the Lord of Salvation to enter into and come out of woman (Mary). Now because the fall was needed to fulfill the blessing God gave to Adam and Eve, that is to say be fruitful. This is True because Our Lord Jesus said the seed must in itself die to become fruitful. He gave us the Truth and He heard it of His Father (Holy Spirit). Nevertheless, we All are born in death, Adam's death, yet because Our Lord Entered it also, it then became away to Life (though you are dead, yet shall you live by me, saith Our Lord Christ Jesus). And those for whom Jesus said were Manifestations of God, the same are of the First fruits .Those that were sent of God, even while Satan cast out of Heaven the host that were trodden under foot, even while he was in Heaven. And of these Righteous, by the firstborn, even as Abel became Righteous, to say the blessing of God the Father of Creation. Yea, Christ came not for them for they were and are in Him because God gave them to Him from the beginning. He came for those who were fallen from deception, not those who were sent (Given Him), even from the beginning (First fruits).Yet, Jesus said that He would turn None Away who come to Him, even the Righteous (those who know Him) saying He came for the sake of the fallen, yet those who were given Him (Sent) they would be drawn to Him by the Father. Adam and Eve were blessed of God(Creator), Adam being the Father of All flesh, and Eve being the Mother of All Living, this meaning that Heaven would Grow, even as Jesus said when He would liken Heaven as something small that Grows to something Very, Very Large. Those of the First Resurrection, which the thousand (1,000) year Millennium is a part and during this time they will multiply (Live more than one Name). These were received into the Kingdom of God (Heavenly Kingdom) and their fruit has remained. This time and season before us, the same is indeed the Last Days. Not that of the First Resurrection, but rather the Last. And it too can come before you and be yet unseen. To this cause you Must look in Spirit or else you will not see that this Message of the Gospel is truly the Glory of the Lord coming and is come, even the clouds of Heaven. And here is where the saying is true; And Son of Man will be seen coming in the clouds of Heaven in His Glory. Yet, to others He will come as a thief in the Night. For this time spoken of is the Rapture which the World sees not, but the children (Remnant of Her seed, Church) will see as the Spirit Reveals it unto them, because they do hunger for Him, even as it is written ; And He said unto His disciples, the days will come, when _ye_ _shall_ _desire_ to _see_ one of the days of the _Son_ _of_ _Man_, And _ye_ _shall_ _not_ _see_ it. And they shall say to you, see here; or see there: go not after them nor follow them. For _as_ the _Lightning_, that _Lightenth_ out of the _One_ _Part_ _Under_ _Heaven_, _Shineth_ unto the _Other_ _Part_ _Under_ _heaven;_ so shall also the _Son_ _of_ _Man_ _be_ _in_ _His_ _Day_. Therefore those that hunger for Him in their spirit shall see His Glory and their ear shall hear His Voice and they shall be caught up in the clouds with Him, Yea even the dead in Christ. But those who worship Him in vain, the same shall not see Him coming in the clouds of Heaven and will not hear His Voice, for He will be to them as a thief in the night, because they hunger not for Him, but rather desire to honour themselves in His Name and will not understand this which is written concerning the Lord's servants; So likewise ye, when ye shall have done All those things which are commanded you, say, we are unprofitable servants: We have done that which was our duty to do. Yea, they that do worship the Lord in vain seeking to honor themselves first and the Lord after themselves, by reason of the words they speak in their heart. For they do say; Lord <u>we</u> cast out devils in your Name, rather then say; Lord Your Name cast out devils when we should speak it before them. Again I say these who seek their own glory will not see the Rapture, nor will they understand that which the Lord said unto the seventy; I beheld Satan as Lightning fall from Heaven. Behold, I give unto you Power to tread on serpents and scorpion, and over All the power of the enemy: And nothing shall by any means hurt you. Notwithstanding in this Rejoice Not, that spirits are subject unto you; but rather Rejoice, because your names are written in Heaven. He who has an ear, let him hear and understand. The servant who humbles himself and glories in the Lord, shall hear the Lord and see His Glory and shall Rejoice in Spirit. And the servant who glories himself in the Name of the Lord, knows Not the Master, nor His Ways of Life. And to this cause he will glory in his own self-righteousness, which is All he will see and will follow death because the spirit that he serves has exalted himself before God and is Now cast down. To this cause All this servant shall hear is the voice of self-deception which glories itself before the Lord. Oh Little Ones both small and great, hear what the Spirit of Truth has said; There are doctrine and sayings in the midst of you that have blinded your fathers before you and their ears unlike yours could not hear. For the First Resurrection was to make just men perfect unto Righteousness and to Redeem those who cameforth from the Millennium and thereby being the Resurrection of Righteousness unto the world. And the Second Resurrection which is a Short season, the Resurrection of damnation, even unto the Father of Lies, who in these days must be Revealed. For God sealed him unto this time and season, for surly he is raised up (Released) in the Resurrection of damnation in the Last Days. Fear not Oh Little Ones, be of good cheer. For the Rapture is come unto you, even in the days he appears (the Evil One). Yea, the Lord Jesus Receives you even when the world (unbelievers) are not able to see. For All they (the world) can see is the God of the Earth come unto them, who has already closed their ears and made their eyes unable to see. For they are willing to consider the First Resurrection as yet coming that their works and deeds might be concealed. Surly they Glorify themselves in the Name of the Lord Jesus Christ, but they do err and worship His Name in Vain. For they know Him not, if they can not hear Him as He speaks in this the Last Days. For the Holy Spirit, even the Spirit of Truth takes that which is the Lord's (even as He had said while He was yet presently with us) and reveals it unto the Little Ones (Remnant of her seed, Church) and the same are a body of Peoples. Not Assembled into One Congregation, but rather One Spirit, that is to say, Christ Jesus. For this reason did Jesus say that He would Return in the Last Days with His Holy Angels and receive unto Himself All that were given in Him, from one end of heaven to the other. Yet there are those who believe that the First Resurrection is yet unfinished and still a thousand (1,000) years to be fulfilled. For the First Resurrection has come and gone and yet for them it is still unseen. How then shall they see the Second ? If they are Looking for the First Resurrection and the Glory thereof, when the

Second Resurrection is before them; What Glory shall they see ? The Glory of the Second Resurrection is given unto the Man of Sin. For it is his time to be revealed. And to those who can not hear and thereby Not see; they shall have the Great Delusion sent by God and in it shall believe that the Millennium is come before them and Receive this Man of Sin. And he shall bring his false peace with him, for it is his Glory and his Light from the beginning. Yea, the Shining One is He. And Great is His Darkness, yet unto the World, it shall appear as a Great Light. Yea, in this day, the Church (Remnant of her seed) shall have already been taken away, Received of the Lord. This being the sixty-fold (60) and what remains are the two (2) witnesses and the thirty-fold (30) that shall hear them and give the God of Heaven and Earth Glory; they being the Remnant of Cain's seed. Then shall the seventh trump be heard and the Brightness of God Almighty is come, even so Father.

Amen and Amen.......

And this is the Gospel of the Two Witnesses and their Testimony, for they are made "Alive" by reason of the Rapture: Remember from hence you are fallen and Repent and believe the Gospel. For they that remain after the earth is moved out of her place is the seed of Cain. For those that are Asleep in Christ before the Rapture are Awakened just before the earth is troubled and enter into Christ. This being the sixty-fold (60). Behold, look about you for the Holy Spirit has Awakened Many. You need not understand the Mystery of God to be Awakened (saved). Only to believe in Christ Jesus as the Son of God and to desire to Love even as He Loves. For the understanding of the Mystery is given to the few, yet Faith is given to the Many. Yea, it is Faith that is Able to Save you,. Faith of Christ Jesus the Lord of Lords and King of Kings, even so Father.

Amen.......

Now after the Rapture and the earth is moved out of her place the two witnesses shall speak unto the thirty-fold (30), that they might Remember and enter in for they too are Asleep in Christ, but they must be last and they must go through Great Tribulation before they are able to enter in. And the Lord said; the servant that Knows his Lord's will and prepares Not himself, shall be beaten with many stripes. But he that Knew Not, and did commit things worthy of stripes, shall be beaten with few stripes. For unto whomsoever much is given, of him shall be much required. Yea, those of the Second Resurrection are of the other flock which Our Lord did speak of at the end or Last Days of His Ministry. Indeed, of those that walk in these Last Days, there are those who Know that Christ Jesus is Lord and thereby Know His Will, but they will not believe this is the time and to this cause they will not enter in and partake of the Rapture, but must go through Great Tribulation, even the thirty-fold (30). And of those who believe, they will prepare themselves by Knowing that the signs and wonders of this time and season are true and they enter therein. And eat Again the Lord's flesh and drink Again the Lord's blood. For they are those who have remained and are "Alive". The same shall speak to those that are Asleep in Christ, even the final hour of the Rapture, and to these that sleep, the same are they that Know Not the Lord's Will, but do things worthy of stripes. Yet, shall be beaten with few stripes. To whom Much is given, much is required. And to whom Little is given, little is required. He who has an ear to hear and a heart that understands, take hold of these sayings. To Know the Will of the Lord of Glory, you must eat His flesh, indeed. For this is His Life He Lived as a man and gave as an example that we might desire and seek to do Likewise. That is to say, Learn of Him and hunger for Him. And Likewise you must drink His blood, indeed. For this is His doctrine, which was given Him of the Father for us, that we might be Reproved of sin and of Righteousness and of Judgment. This is to say, Learn of His teachings And of His Mighty Works. For His Mighty Works came by reason of His doctrine. And His doctrine came by reason of His Father. For so it seemed good in the sight of the Heavenly Father to give All Power and All Authority unto the Son of God, because He was also Son of Man. Therefor All things shall be subjected to Him and put under Him, even the Father. For the Father's Will is done, even so:

Amen.......

Now of these that Know the Lord's Will and do prepare themselves, let this not trouble you, for they are the same that partook of the First Resurrection and entered into the Second Resurrection because God the Son has sent them. To this cause are they made Able to prepare themselves. This is not done of flesh, but rather Spirit. If any man Trust himself, he is a fool. And if any man Trust God, he is wise. And if a deceitful man requires you to trust God so that he himself can gain of you, then his Life shall be the cost of his deceitfulness and his only increase is a greater damnation. Or if he is a brethren who has fallen away and has become blinded in his way. Then he is in danger of losing his fruitfulness and shall enter into judgment, which will bring many sorrows and should he repent of it and return unto the truth, then he will find his joy and he will give alms of such as he has and all things shall be restored unto him. And because you were willing to Trust God rather than distrust the man. Your increase shall be Life Everlasting, And if you truly have Trusted God, then when you find (see) the deceitfulness of the man, you will not have <u>revenge</u> for him, but rather <u>pray</u> for him. That he too might find forgiveness in his heart from God. And if you can not find forgiveness in your heart for this man, then you must pray unto the Father in the Name of Christ Jesus that you might find this forgiveness in you, which is from the Lord.. For to Trust God truly is to believe and thereby find His Forgiveness in you. Brethren, you can not always find this forgiveness <u>instantly</u>, but you <u>shall always find it</u>. Knock and the door shall be opened. Do good works not for yourself, but for others and give God the Glory. Be slow to anger and quick to forgive and love one another as Christ has Loved you. Therefore pray always for the Brethren. This is the way and this is the Light that the Lord of Heaven and Earth did give us to do. Even so Oh Holy One thy Spirit is One and thy Will is done.

Amen and Amen.......

~ Endword ~

Daniel 2:20-22

20 Daniel answered and said, Blessed be the name of God for ever and ever: for wisdom and might are his: 21 And he <u>changeth</u> the <u>times</u> and the <u>seasons</u>: he removeth kings, and setteth up kings: he giveth wisdom unto the wise, and knowledge to them that know understanding: 22 He <u>revealeth</u> the <u>deep</u> and <u>secret</u> things: he knoweth what is <u>in the</u> <u>darkness</u>, and the <u>light dwelleth with him</u>.

Behold, I give you a Truth. The One spoken of here is The Holy Ghost even the Spirit of Truth. He is the Alpha and Omega. The Beginning and the End. He is the Movement over the Face of the Waters. He is The Great I am. Praise be to God, for His work is done in us and we are made able to see. That we should give Him the Glory and this makes us witnesses of the things that must be, to fulfill the Words of God. For He is God and All that He Says "Must" come to pass. And there are those on High who are given Wisdom and others given Knowledge. And there are places on the earth where there is Power and Strength by reason of understandings. And there are the Fowl of Heaven that must appear and dwell among us if the Word of God should be fulfilled. And with them comes the evidence of this testament. And also the answer to the question; where then did the fall come from? It came from The Cherub who covers. Known to us as the Serpent and the Devil. And through the High Ones of Old, spoken of in Daniel as the fourth beast which was more diversed then the other beasts. Even a Nation. Daniel 7:19.

Amen......

This time before us is not the End, but the beginning of the End of time as we know it. Yet there is enough left to make up a life time for some. Therefore take hold of this Truth and let it be your guide as to how you should live this time which remains. Learn of Christ as He is and not how others would have you to believe Him to be. His words remain with us, even to this day. And the Holy Spirit likewise. Therefore, eat of His flesh and drink His blood and let the Holy Spirit Reveal Him unto your heart. He will gather some of you together for fellowship in His Name. And others, He will have you to go here and there for His Name sake and this will be your <u>workship</u> for Him. Nevertheless, let not your heart be troubled as to the events that are forth-coming and be not afraid for your life, because He will keep you and not let you be harmed. If this Truth finds you after the Rapture. Let not your thought be: If it were true then it is too late for me. And you have only one life to live and you should take what you can or you will have nothing to show for it. Then the other lie would be: Eat,

69

drink and be merry, for tomorrow you shall die. Let not fear or hopelessness deceive you that you should become offended and lose sight of the Truth. For Woe unto the world for offenses, but the world needs offenses that your heart should be tried and found to have Christ in-dwelling, but first you must eat of Him and drink of Him. Then He is found in you and you shall endure and not faint, because He will walk with-in you, with you. This is the Truth and the Life which He spoke about while He was presently with us. He will Never leave you alone nor will He forsake you. Just learn of Him and call on His Name and He will do the rest with you and for you, because He is Son of Man and you are His man child. Love Him as He loves you. Just try to be like Him. It is enough to be as your Lord.

Amen and Amen.......